"Jeff Dodge is one of the most ⌐ ⌐, ⌐ ⌐ has led countless people to Christ, discipling them in the way of Jesus. This book will equip the church to carry out our mission by taking us through a clear, easy-to-understand layout of the language of the gospel. By the end of this book you will feel less scared and more confident to share the gospel with those around you, including those who seem really hostile to the faith. The Great Commission starts with getting the gospel right, and this book gets the gospel right. Read and go do likewise."

Russell Moore, President, Ethics & Religious Liberty Commission of the Southern Baptist Convention

"Jeff is a thought leader as it relates to gospel-centered ministry in the context of the local church. I'm so thankful that he has written this rich and accessible introduction to the gospel and the implications of the gospel. It will undoubtedly serve the church for years to come."

J. T. English, Pastor of the Village Church Institute,

"I first came across Jeff Dodge's gospel training course more than a decade ago when a college student passed a copy along to me. I've referred to it often since then—in fact, it's sitting in a binder on my bookshelf right now! I'm thrilled to see this excellent resource published. It will help you understand the gospel more fully and communicate it to others more effectively."

Bob Thune, Founding Pastor, Coram Deo Church, Omaha, NE; author of *Gospel Eldership* and coauthor of *The Gospel-Centered Life*

"For over a decade *Gospel 101* has deeply impacted college students and leaders planting churches in university connects. It has given emerging leaders enormous clarity in understanding Christ, his work, his mission and his call for Christ followers to make disciples. Dodge's simple, transferable insights drive to the heart of mission, giving readers a clear pathway for advancing God's Kingdom through how they think, how they live, and how they articulate the gospel to the lost. I recommend this book because I like it, but even more because I see the fruit of its impact."

Brian N. Frye, National Collegiate Strategist, North American Mission Board

"Jeff Dodge is one of the most vibrant followers of Christ and one of the most committed Christian ministers I know. He also serves one of the most compelling college ministries I've ever observed. He is a man worth listening to, and *Gospel 101* is a book I highly recommend reading."

Jason K. Allen, President of Midwestern Baptist Theological Seminary

"*Gospel 101* is a primer on the gospel. It covers the theological and biblical basics, but always with an eye toward evangelism and how to share the message that changes our lives. Jeff Dodge brings simplicity, clarity, and passion to the central message of the Bible and showcases Jesus as the Hero of the story."

Trevin Wax, Director for Bibles and Reference at LifeWay Christian Resources; author of *This Is Our Time* and *Eschatological Discipleship*

"Of all the messages competing for our attention today, none is more needed than the gospel. With more than 267 million people in North America headed to an eternity separated from God, we need men and women who can confidently share the gospel with the people God is bringing into their lives. My friend Jeff Dodge's book, *Gospel 101*, will help you dive deep into how the Bible explains the gospel so you can share it in a simple yet powerful way. I pray as men and women gather to study God's Word through this book, God will use it to begin a gospel movement across North America and the world."

Kevin Ezell, President, North American Mission Board, SBC

GOSPEL 101

GOSPEL 101:
Learning, Living, and Sharing the Gospel

Jeff Dodge

New
Growth
Press
newgrowthpress.com

New Growth Press, Greensboro, NC 27401
newgrowthpress.com
Copyright © 2018 by Jeff Dodge

Cover Design: Faceout Books, faceoutstudio.com
Interior Typesetting and eBook: Lisa Parnell, lparnell.com

ISBN: 978-1-948130-10-3 (print)
ISBN: 978-1-948130-09-7 (ebook)

Printed in India

29 28 27 26 25 24 23 22   5 6 7 8 9

This book is dedicated to
the incredible young men and women
of The Salt Company at Iowa State University.
You continue to prove that the gospel of Jesus Christ
transforms lives and changes the world.

CONTENTS

Expectations

- Do lesson before each class
- Survey at least one person over the course of the 8 sessions. Must be an unbeliever.
- Participate in discussion

What's my testimony? What did I used to think the gospel was?

- "HELL HOUSES"
- Dying & leaving Earth

By the end of this course, a person is more than equipped to share the gospel. You don't have to be an expert!

Introduction

"I watched in dismay as a friend attempted to explain his faith to an unbeliever. As he jumped back and forth from Old Testament to New Testament he used a multitude of verses, but never explained clearly how to become a Christian. Since then I have made a commitment that whatever I do in evangelism, I will never be fuzzy or unclear. I don't have the right to take a simple message and make it difficult."[1]

I read this quote years ago in an article about evangelism, and it has stuck with me ever since. As I think about gospel conversations I have had, it seems there are two ditches I inadvertently fall into. Maybe you can relate.

Information overload. One ditch I fall into is overwhelming my unbelieving friend with content. By the time I am done, I have often felt like I dumped a jigsaw puzzle onto the table and carefully explained a bunch of individual pieces while never actually letting my friend see how beautiful the big picture is—how it all fits together.

Too simplistic. The ditch on the other side is just as dangerous. In my desire to make the gospel understandable (and avoid the first ditch!), I am tempted to reduce the gospel down to quick soundbites, often with Christian jargon that is lost on my unbelieving friend.

The first ditch makes the gospel too complex and leaves my friend lost in data. The other ditch makes the gospel too thin and leaves my friend imagining that the gospel is shallow or even trivial.

We have to avoid those ditches!

THIS IS BECAUSE EXPLAINING THE GOSPEL IS EXPLAINING CHRISTIANITY, WHICH IS BOTH SIMPLE & COMPLEX.

WHICH DITCH DO YOU TEND TO FALL INTO?

1

We must communicate the gospel in a way that acknowledges its profound depth while simultaneously making the message clear, understandable, and compelling. To help you get there, I have three objectives:

> *Gospel Fluency.* You will become familiar with the language of the gospel. We will all spend a lifetime exploring the many dimensions and textures of the gospel, but this book's focus will be on the "big picture" (the core message) of the gospel.

+ Gospel Transformation

> *Gospel Community.* Working through this material with others will add dimension and conviction to your studies. It is amazing what your fellow students will teach you!

> *Gospel Action.* The gospel message is not simply to be studied; it is to be shared. This material will help you engage in gospel conversations with your unbelieving friends and family.

So, grab your Bible (it's going to be your main textbook!), gather a small group of study partners, and use this small group resource as a guide to compel you toward understanding the gospel. You and the others in your small group will emerge from this study not with a formula, but rather new language and new terminology you can use to anchor everyday conversations back to the gospel.

I expect that this coordinated pursuit will lead you to vigorously share this good news with the waiting world!

HOW TO USE THESE SESSIONS

Studying the Bible in community is important. Why? One reason is that if you only study your Bible alone it will be easy for you to go in the wrong direction. We don't self-correct very well. Throughout the centuries, God has used his people to anchor one another in the Scriptures. God has connected us to each other through the Spirit to bring balance and help to our understanding. Because of that, the reading

NOT A FORMULA, BUT A STUDY.

DOES IT FEEL SCARY SHARING THE GOSPEL? WHY? WHY DO YOU THINK WE FEEL SO MUCH PRESSURE?

and activities in each session are designed to be preparation for a small-group discussion. *Complete the study on your own before your group meets.*

Each study starts with a *Bible reading assignment* that will encourage you to engage the text as you answer questions. This is far and away the most important aspect of this study. Then, you will read a short *article* that locates the Bible reading in a broader stream of understanding on that topic. Using what you learned from the Bible passages and the article, you can then complete a short *workbook*.

To finish your preparation, you will be encouraged to conduct a *survey* in order to take what you are learning out into your world. This survey includes a single question you can ask someone in order to get into a spiritual conversation. We suggest taking these surveys to people with whom you have a relationship so that these conversations can develop over the eight sessions of material. Listen and learn from your respondents and watch as you are able to connect the material from this book and your small-group discussions to those conversations. That is gospel fluency in action!

When you meet with your small group, share what you learned from the survey. You may want to compile and compare the group's results. Then use the workbook questions you answered to guide the rest of the discussion.

This book will present the core tenets of the gospel message, invite you to entertain the difficult questions inherent in gospel theology, and get you started on developing your own ways to share your faith with others.

Diving into deep study of the gospel encourages humility. In turn, humility puts us in the right mind frame for worshiping God. Also, this humble posture is just where we need to be as we share our faith with others. As you work through this book, let the gospel truths go deep into your soul. Stop often to praise God in gratitude, and let your joy

STOP FOR MOMENTS OF
REFLECTION TO LET THESE TRUTHS SINK IN.

overflow to others. Studying the gospel necessarily leads to worship, as the apostle Paul illustrates in his letter to the Romans. After writing eleven chapters unpacking the gospel, it is as though he pushes back from his desk, throws his hands in the air, and with tearful joy exclaims,

> Oh, the depth of the riches
> both of the wisdom and of the knowledge of God!
> How unsearchable his judgments
> and untraceable his ways!
> For who has known the mind of the Lord?
> Or who has been his counselor?
> And who has ever given to God,
> that he should be repaid?
> For from him and through him
> and to him are all things.
> To him be the glory forever. Amen. (Romans 11:33–36)

Session

1

"Describe the gospel in one sentence. THE GOSPEL is _____ ="

GOSPEL

WHY THE GOSPEL MATTERS

The word *gospel* is used a lot by Christians. Yet we often use the word without setting it in its proper context. We must begin understanding the gospel by considering how the Bible explains it. The gospel is so central to the Bible that we find the first whispers of it in the opening pages of Genesis and continue to see it unfold until we get to the final words of the last book in the Bible, the book of Revelation.

The gospel is not just all over the Bible; it is all around us. The reason we can talk freely to people about the gospel is because all of us intuitively connect with it—even before we know what "it" is. Think about it: we have this nagging feeling that there is something beyond the material world. Why is that a common phenomenon? We crave hope and promise for a better tomorrow. We long for pure, unconditional love and are brokenhearted when it escapes us. Universally, humanity is hardwired to seek answers only the gospel provides. We even have an innate desire to be rescued by a king. What's with that?

STOP HERE. WHAT DO YOU THINK THAT MEANS?

Don't believe me? Trace the storyline of your favorite movies, the theme of the songs on your go-to playlist, or even the simplest bedtime stories. We can't escape it. Is it possible that we fill our screens and earbuds with stories that point us to *the Story*—the gospel? Many of the stories we love, the aspirations that drive us, and even the heartbreaks that haunt

5

We're narrative creatures

us all form the shadow of a greater Story. And maybe if we heard *the Story*—the gospel—we would recognize it and embrace it.

We hope *Gospel 101* just seems to make sense. Nothing new. Nothing novel. It is actually incredibly familiar. It is intended to bring clarity to the Story that is central to the Bible and uniquely makes sense of the world. And one more thing (spoiler alert): the hero king at the center of it is Jesus.

* * *

To prepare for your small group meeting:

- Complete the reading assignment
- Read the article
- Answer the workbook questions
- Survey three people

READING ASSIGNMENT

Read through the passages below a minimum of three times. Use a different translation each time. Record your observations below.

NOTE: Though there are many good translations to choose from, let me offer a few suggestions to get you started. For a translation that works hard to stay as close as possible to a word-for-word translation from the original languages into English, start with the English Standard Bible (ESV) or the New American Standard Bible (NASB). For a translation that focuses on making the English more readable, try the Christian Standard Bible (CSB), which is the one I use in this book, or the New International Version (NIV). For a paraphrase Bible that works even harder on making the text readable for the English reader, start with the New Living Translation (NLT).

What does each text tell me about the gospel or *good news*?

- Romans 1:1–17 and 6:20–23

- 1 Corinthians 15:1–8

- Revelation 14:6–7

Session

ARTICLE

Headlines are important. Some are even epic and timeless, especially if the headline is followed by news that rivets and changes the world. For instance, a headline declaring "PEACE!" grabs the attention of every reader who is ravaged by a devastating war. Context is everything with headlines.

The gospel stands as the Bible's attention-getting headline of good news. In fact, the word *gospel* literally means "GOOD NEWS!" The story that follows the headline tells the reader that Jesus Christ, the Son of God, has come to set us free from sin by his life, death, and resurrection. That headline should grab the attention of every human being. But does it?

The goal of *Gospel 101* is to set the headline of the gospel in its context—to answer the question, "What is the gospel?" If we ignore the backstory, we will certainly not be riveted by the headline.

I first started thinking about the need to understand the bigger context of the gospel when I read an intriguing passage in the last book of the Bible, the book of Revelation (which then sent me to the opening pages of the *first* book of the Bible—but more on that later). "Then I saw another angel flying high overhead, with the eternal gospel to announce to the inhabitants of the earth—to every nation, tribe, language, and people. He spoke with a loud voice: 'Fear God and give him glory, because the hour of his judgment has come. Worship the one who made heaven and earth, the sea and the springs of water'" (Revelation 14:6–7).

[handwritten margin note:] If Christianity starts to feel like bad news, then something is off...

8

That passage really caught my attention. First, it is the only time God sends an angel to globally declare the big headline—the eternal gospel. But isn't there something glaringly missing? "Um, Mr. Angel, sir, I don't want to sound impolite. I mean, I'm from Iowa and you're, well, an angel. But didn't you leave something out? More to the point, didn't you leave some*one* out—Jesus, for instance?"

I panned back and looked at the context of this passage and was reminded that Jesus Christ is the central figure in the book of Revelation. The whole book is "the revelation of Jesus Christ" (Revelation 1:1). It is not lost on the angel that Jesus is the centerpiece of the gospel message. But in chapter 14, the angel proclaims aspects of the eternal gospel that are often missed. The angel declares a gospel that is centered on the Creator who is coming to judge the inhabitants of the earth—every nation, tribe, language, and people. By qualifying the gospel with the word *eternal,* the angel is telling us there is something timeless about this good news.

Then it hit me: the angel at the *very end* of the Bible is telling us that the eternal gospel starts at the *very beginning* of the Bible—the story of creation. The gospel is the storyline that ties the whole Bible together! This sent me on a journey to understand the incredible backstory of the gospel.

God isn't coy or unclear about this storyline. I think I had just been reading too fast to see it. In fact, here are a few of the cover-to-cover aspects of the gospel's backstory that became clearer and made Jesus's role in the gospel all the more incredible.

[handwritten margin notes: "THE ETERNAL GOSPEL = THE STORY OF REALITY FROM BEGINNING TO END"; "3 OVERVIEW CONCEPTS"]

1. THE ETERNAL GOSPEL IS THE TRUE STORY OF GOD'S KINGDOM

The angel's eternal gospel concisely focuses our eyes on the God of the universe and specifically on his role as Creator. The creation-focused language the angel uses takes us from the final book of the Bible back to the beginning of the Bible in the book of Genesis.

Consider all of creation as God's kingdom realm. This kingdom theme is prevalent page after page and culminates in the crowning of Jesus as the supreme King of all at the end of Revelation.

THE STORY ENDS W/ JESUS' CORONATION

When an author reveals a theme that can be traced from the opening pages and ties it all the way to the concluding pages, that is probably something the reader should take note of! The Bible was written by many different human authors over thousands of years, and yet there remains a cohesive and distinct plotline. Make no mistake: the true Author of Scripture intentionally wove everything together for our sake.

Many authors, playwrights, and screenwriters follow a storyline similar to what we see in the Bible. We recognize it and connect to it. Check it out:

- First, there is the description of a kingdom marked by peace, harmony, and life-as-it-should-be that is disrupted suddenly and catastrophically. The kingdom falls into enemy hands (Genesis 1–3).
- The plot thickens and grows in intensity until the hero-king appears to reckon with the enemy. This is the apex of the story, accompanied by significant conflict and ultimate, heroic victory (Genesis 4–Revelation 20).
- Finally, peace and harmony and life-as-it-should-be is reestablished in the kingdom due to the heroism of the hero-king (Revelation 21–22).

It is as if God has put an antenna in us to pick up the signals pointing us to this epic storyline. As we go about our lives on this earth, we intuitively know something is very wrong. We long for peace and for a kingdom to be restored. God has written this epic narrative and the traces of it are all around us.

THE GARDEN = WALLED PARADISE (JUST LIFE + KINGDOM)

PROBLEM → CLIMAX → RESOLUTION

DISCUSSION QUESTION:

WHAT'S HARD FOR US TO UNDERSTAND ABOUT THE KINGDOM THEME?

1. ESTABLISHMENT OF KINGDOM
2. FALLEN KINGDOM
3. THE PROMISED & LONG-AWAITED KING COMES
4. THE KINGDOM IS RESTORED

2. THE ETERNAL GOSPEL CENTERS ON THE TRUE HERO-KING, JESUS

The coming of a hero-king was the long-awaited hope of God's kingdom since Genesis 3 (more on that in the next lesson). When Jesus stepped onto the scene, a booming voice from heaven announced his royal entrance. Immediately, Jesus began to declare the headline: "The time is fulfilled, and the kingdom of God has come near. Repent and believe the good news!" (Mark 1:15).

The apostle Paul picks up on the theme as he instructs the church in Rome about the eternal gospel. Paul alerts the reader about the overarching storyline of the Bible and zeroes in on Jesus's role as hero. Notice how he begins and concludes his letter with this theme.

> Paul, a servant of Christ Jesus, called as an apostle and set apart for the gospel of God—*which he promised beforehand through his prophets in the Holy Scriptures*—concerning his Son, *Jesus Christ our Lord*, who was a descendant of David according to the flesh and was appointed to be the powerful Son of God according to the Spirit of holiness by the resurrection of the dead. Through him we have received grace and apostleship to bring about the obedience of faith for the sake of his name among all the Gentiles. (Romans 1:1–5, emphasis added)

> Now to him who is able to strengthen you according to my gospel and the proclamation about Jesus Christ, *according to the revelation of the mystery kept silent for long ages but now revealed and made known through the prophetic Scriptures,* according to the command of the eternal God to advance the obedience of faith among all the Gentiles—to the only wise God, *through Jesus Christ*—to him be the glory forever! Amen. (Romans 16:25–27, emphasis added)

This gospel message is present in the storyline from the first page until the last. The message itself is about the hero-king Jesus Christ, the Son of God as confirmed by his resurrection and by the testimony of the Holy Spirit.

Do you sense the urgency? Humanity has fallen, and the earth is not as it should be. But, the King has returned to his kingdom. All who hear should heed!

3. THE ETERNAL GOSPEL CALLS FOR A RESPONSE

Remember that *gospel* simply means "good news." It is *news*, a message we are to proclaim to all people. And it is *good* because the King in whose realm we live is coming and he wants us to know him and enjoy him forever. This news is not just informational, it anticipates action!

What response is Jesus after? Look at Mark 1:15 above. Jesus calls for *repentance and belief.* Also look again at the two passages from Romans above. Paul refers to the response as "the obedience of faith" at both the beginning and the end of his letter.

Because humanity has fallen, our inherited state is one of desperate need. When we hear this message about Jesus Christ, we will either choose to repent and believe or we will choose to deny our King and suffer the consequences. There is no in-between. And as we do follow him in the joyful obedience of faith, we find new life in him. We live as citizens of his kingdom!

One way we serve as citizens is as bearers of his message: *Hear ye, hear ye, the long-awaited kingdom is dawning.*[2] Again, the apostle Paul picks up on this aspect of the eternal gospel, reminding his readers that there is an urgency to proclaiming the gospel. "How, then, can they call on him they have not believed in? And how can they believe without hearing about him? And how can they hear without a preacher? And how

We must first live as citizens before we urge others to do the same.

can they preach unless they are sent? As it is written: 'How beautiful are the feet of those who bring good news.' But not all obeyed the gospel. For Isaiah says, 'Lord, who has believed our message?' So faith comes from what is heard, and what is heard comes through the message about Christ" (Romans 10:14–17).

Can someone pick up a Bible, read it on their own, and come to know Christ? Conceivably. Yet, if you think about your own life, I would bet that you can trace your journey of faith back to a relationship with a believer who told you the gospel. "Faith comes from what is heard." Those gospel pamphlets left in the public restroom—not compelling! Instead, God calls Christians to use their feet and their voices to proclaim the gospel. This is how this glorious message has spread across the world.

The story of a kingdom that needs to be rescued & restored by its long-awaited King, Jesus. It calls for a response: repent & believe!

APPLICATION

This is only a brief introduction to the gospel, but I hope you are already captivated by the beauty of this message and its hero, Jesus. If you have already repented and believed this gospel and are now seeking to proclaim this message to others, your Bible study and the session above have provided you plenty of content to begin to do just that! In your home, you can remind your family how the struggles of your day are very real—but are ultimately resolved by our true King. As you seek community with other Christians, you can remind each other that your decision to follow Christ was a decision to eternally give him his proper due as a King, and you can ask if there are any areas of your life that don't demonstrate your King's influence. In your classroom or your workplace, you can agree with your peers that the world is indeed as broken as it seems, and yet "the kingdom of God is near. Repent and believe the good news!"

All of us can declare: Jesus is the answer!

It's a simple message!

1. What did you learn about the gospel from your reading assignment? How has your understanding of the gospel been challenged?

2. What is simple about the gospel? What is complex or confusing about the gospel? Why is it important to understand both the simplicity and the complexity of the gospel?

3. Why is the question "What is the gospel?" so difficult? If someone now asked you that question, how would you answer it?

4. The article highlighted three overarching principles in considering the theology of the gospel. Fill in the blanks below to test yourself.

The eternal gospel _____

_____

The eternal gospel _____

_____

The eternal gospel _____

_____

5. Which of these principles resonates with you the most? Why?

6. Why do Christians often fail to talk about Jesus with the same eagerness they might share other good news? What does the Bible have to say that might address a believer's fears and insecurities in talking about Jesus?

SURVEY

Survey three people.

ASK: Have you ever read the Bible? What is the main message of the Bible?

RESPONSE FROM PERSON #1:

RESPONSE FROM PERSON #2:

RESPONSE FROM PERSON #3:

NOTE FOR YOURSELF: What did you learn from your survey? What connections do you see between the survey responses and the article or the Scriptures you've been studying?

SMALL GROUP MEETING

Meet with your group to share what you learned from the survey and discuss your workbook answers.

2

GOD

WHY STARTING WITH GOD MATTERS

Sometimes our impressions of people are way off. For instance, have you ever met someone after a friend has told you all about them, only to discover they were nothing like your friend described? There is nothing like actually getting to know someone for yourself. Giving people the opportunity to introduce themselves is far better than taking others' words for it.

When it comes to God, we have heard a lot about him. People have all sorts of ideas and opinions about God. Some are valid. Some are way off. How can we know what is true?

We should let God introduce himself to us.

God actually does a pretty remarkable job of telling us about himself in the opening pages of the Bible. There are some things he absolutely wants us to know right off. Our impression of who God is should be shaped by God—not by what others have surmised about God (whether good or bad). More, God sets the stage for the entirety of his book in these opening pages. We can't skip too quickly past these all-important pages.

I will go further: nothing else about God, the Bible, or the central message of the eternal gospel will make sense if we do not take the time to let God set the stage for us in the opening pages of his book. God may not be exactly as you may have imagined. Others may have tainted your impression of him. Take your time. Let God introduce himself to you.

Student, I'd like to introduce you to God.

God, is there anything you'd like us to know about you?

**

To prepare for your small group meeting:

- Complete the reading assignment
- Read the article
- Answer the workbook questions
- Survey three people

READING ASSIGNMENT

Read Genesis 1–3 a minimum of three times. Use a different translation each time. Read deliberately and inquisitively. Record your observations below.

- What does this text tell me about God?

- What does this text tell me about humanity?

Session

ARTICLE

2

A story is headed somewhere.

If you are reading a story, it's hard to make sense of it unless you understand the plot. You need to understand who the main characters are and where the whole story is going. That is also true of the story of our lives! If we don't understand the main characters in our own story, we have no hope of understanding ourselves or our world. The gospel starts at the beginning of the Bible and gives us the overarching narrative of our lives. Perhaps surprisingly, it turns out that the main character is not a human. The main character of our story is not us—it is God.

In the opening pages of Genesis, we get an enthralling account of God calling his world into existence and creating his most precious creation, human beings. The true story of who God is and how he made us sets the stage for the rest of the story of the gospel to unfold.

GOD: LOVING CREATOR

It is easy to read quickly through the opening of Genesis and miss something significant. God had a blank canvas to work with. No obstacles. No constraints. No blueprint to follow. He could have done anything! It follows, then, that what he did was one hundred percent intentional!

God created *ex nihilo*, "out of nothing." God spoke the word and creation snapped into existence. It is breathtaking to imagine! Then, before the newly created sun set on the sixth day, God hit pause and rolled up his sleeves for his crowning achievement—the creation of the first man and woman. But he didn't just speak them into existence; he "formed"

Adam with his own hands and "breathed the breath of life into his nostrils" (Genesis 2:7). Likewise, he personally crafted Eve—forming her from a rib of Adam's. God displayed his love for Adam and Eve through his tenderness and nearness to both of them. And he continued to pour out his love on them after he created them.

Consider the incredible home God set up for them. God went far beyond giving them what they needed to survive. The Garden of Eden was a place of beauty and lushness. There were flowering trees, plentiful resources, biological diversity—a place that engaged sight, scent, smell, touch, and taste. You can almost see the loving gaze of God upon humanity in these pages.

Have you ever wondered why God created people? Sometimes we answer that question by saying *for fellowship*. God certainly did enjoy friendship with Adam and Eve, but it's important to remember what the Bible lays out in the creation story: God did not create the world and people to live in it because he was lonely. As the almighty, self-sustaining Creator, God had all he needed, *yet* he chose to create humans in his own image and lavish us with his lovingkindness. *That* is the story. And the centerpiece is God (not you and me!).

Because of his great love, God had a wonderful plan for what humans would do in his newly created world. Look at Genesis 1:26–28.

> Then God said, "Let us make man in our image, according to our likeness. They will rule the fish of the sea, the birds of the sky, the livestock, the whole earth, and the creatures that crawl on the earth."
> So God created man in his own image;
> he created him in the image of God;
> he created them male and female.
> God blessed them, and God said to them, "Be fruitful, multiply, fill the earth, and subdue it. Rule the fish of the sea, the birds of the sky, and every creature that crawls on the earth."

GOD ALSO SAID HIS CREATION WAS GOOD, WHICH INCLUDES HUMANITY. GEN. 1:31

"Rule" = Radah (Heb: `raw-daw`)

SUBDUE = "everything in its proper place." (Jordan Peterson)

Humankind was given the task of *ruling* and *subduing* God's creation. Adam and Eve were to watch over and protect what God had made as his viceroys (see Genesis 2:5, 15). OUR PURPOSE!!!

God gives us dignity by giving us a role to play, we are not powerless.

We don't use the word *viceroy* very often, but it is the perfect word to describe humanity's role in God's world. A viceroy is a governor of a kingdom who rules as the representative of a king. A viceroy does not have inherent authority, but is appointed by a king to be the royal eyes, hands, and feet on the king's behalf. PSALM 8

In Genesis 1, God created and named all the objects he created as an expression of his ownership and kingship. That's why it is so surprising in Genesis 2 when God delegates to Adam, his newly appointed viceroy, the task of naming every living creature (see Genesis 2:19).

God demonstrated his role as loving Creator by entrusting people with incredible authority and the capacity to flourish. What potential there was for the human race! EPH. 2:10

GOD: SUPREME AUTHORITY

OUR ORIGINAL CONDITION

It makes sense to us that we are in charge of what we create. And in Genesis 1–3 we see God demonstrate his supreme authority by ordering creation and humankind as-it-should-be.

As God spoke forth creation, he started with an earth that was formless, empty, and dark (Genesis 1:2). Like a master architect, he began to put things in order. He separated the light from the dark. He created and established boundaries, commanding the water to go here and the land to appear there. Even the Garden of Eden—humanity's perfect kingdom—did not sprawl endlessly but was placed exactly where God wanted it (2:8).

Then, as God created humans as the pinnacle of creation, he also purposefully created them under his authority. Humanity would not be a coruler or equal partner, but rather an executor of the King's

"ANY TREE" - GOD GIVES US MORE THAN ENOUGH TO DELIGHT IN & ENJOY

TRUE FREEDOM HAS LIMITATIONS

already-determined rule (a viceroy). We see this expression of supreme authority over humanity in the brief scene in which God presents the limits of their dominion. "And the LORD God commanded the man, 'You are free to eat from any tree of the garden, but you must not eat from the tree of the knowledge of good and evil, for on the day you eat from it, you will certainly die'" (Genesis 2:16–17).

WE MUST ACCEPT OUR LIMITATIONS.

God lovingly gave humanity amazing freedom and a special place of honor, but there were limits. God had ordered creation perfectly. He was in charge, and *humans would flourish only under this supreme authority.* To go against his will would effectively mean trading life for death.

TO BE FREE, WE MUST SUBMIT.
TO LIVE, WE MUST DIE.

TRANSGRESSING OUR LIMITS IS DISREGARDING GOD'S AUTHORITY IN ORDER TO BE OUR OWN. WE WANT TO MAKE OUR OWN LIMITS.

In God's world and under his authority, Adam and Eve would enjoy a perfect relationship with God and each other. They would know who they were and would express dignity and joy in ruling God's creation. Everything was set up for humans to be much more than survivors— they would thrive under God's loving rule. God's Kingdom was in a state of *Shalom*, life-as-it-should-be.

Yet something was about to go terribly wrong.

Let's take another look at Genesis 1:26–28. We can see that God knew sin and the curses that flow from it were coming. Here is what I mean: the word *rule* in Genesis 1:26 and 28 in its original language of Hebrew is *radah*, which carries the connotation of "oppressing, or ruling by conquering." The word for *subdue* in verse 28 is *kabash*, which means "to force into bondage."

Now wait. Let's think about this. I thought everything was "very good." Why the language of battle and bondage? Indeed, humans were given a special place under God's authority, but they would soon bring this kingdom crashing down.

GOD: FINAL JUDGE

Adam and Eve directly disobeyed God's command. God told them plainly, don't eat from the tree or you will die. Sadly and disastrously, they did it anyway!

Adam and Eve chose independence and their own will over God's protection and care. They chose to turn their backs on God. And as with all choices, there were consequences. God made the world. It belongs to him. The one rule he made for Adam and Eve had been broken. Their desire for independence from the God who created them resulted in sorrow, brokenness, and death.

The consequences were immediate. Now their loving Creator would act as their judge. A judge unwilling to execute justice is, quite simply, *untrustworthy*. It is good, right, and necessary for authority to be expressed in perfect justice—especially when the judge is as extraordinarily loving and benevolent as our Creator!

What were the consequences? For the woman, even the greatest gift— the birth of a child—would come with a painful reminder that all is not as-it-should-be. For the man, the once joyful work of caring for a lush garden would become painful toil. Humans would not live forever. They would literally be worn down to dust. They were once the guardians of the garden. Now? They would be guarded *from* the garden.

Yet, even in the midst of administering perfect justice, God offered hope. As he sentenced the serpent with judgment, we find these words: "I will put hostility between you and the woman, and between your offspring and her offspring. *He will strike your head*, and you will strike his heel" (Genesis 3:15, emphasis added).

The judgment toward humanity for the first sin was heavy. Humans would indeed receive the promised penalty of death. They would no longer reside in the presence of their loving and holy God. Yet in Genesis 3:15 we also see a divine plan introduced that would result in the

Handwritten margin notes:
- GOD'S FIRST & ONLY LAW
- THE FEAR OF GOD IS THE BEGINNING OF WISDOM.
- FROM RULING THE GARDEN TO EXILE FROM THE GARDEN.
- SEPARATED FROM GOD

serpent being CRUSHED. One would arise from humankind—a son of Eve—who would strike the head of the serpent, crushing evil forever. This promise is often called the *protoevangelium*, the "first gospel." Here we get a glimpse of how the story will end: not with God abandoning his broken world, but with a Savior—an offspring of Adam and Eve who would destroy sin and death forever.

The lovingkindness of God, first seen in the tenderness of his touch and the beauty of the garden, would save his rebellious people and restore their honor.

The death sentence would remain in place. Those who deny God's authority would certainly die. But God would also make a way to bring his children home.

APPLICATION

By looking at both the creation and the fall of humankind, we can see a full picture of God's character and the overarching plotline of the Bible—the gospel. God is our loving Creator and also holds final authority over our lives and over everything else he has made. People still attempt to live outside of God's love and authority. The consequences are still dire, but God has provided a way back to him—a way back to thriving as we were created to do. God resolved to save us through his "offspring." This is the God of the gospel. This is the story he has invited us into. This is the message you can bring to others.

As you read and discuss this chapter with your small group, be thinking about how these gospel themes could flow into your conversation. Where do you see in your own life a dislike for God's authority (or anyone else's)? How does this part of the gospel story play out in your home, school, work, and neighborhood? How has it affected our whole world?

Many books have been written about how to fix the problems in our world. But the gospel teaches us that a solution to sorrow, disease, evil, and death must come from outside of ourselves. What gospel hope can you offer to your friends, neighbors, and coworkers this week?

WORKBOOK

2

1. How does God begin his revelation to humanity, the Bible? What elements do you see in this introduction that will be important to understanding the gospel?

2. What three key attributes of God do we see in Genesis 1–3? What other attributes did you note in your reading assignment?

3. Which of these three attributes of God do you tend to minimize? In thinking about your own life, what is the effect of minimizing God in this way?

4. Explain humanity's role as a viceroy. How is understanding this role important in understanding God's relationship to humanity?

5. Based on Genesis 1–3, how does God being our supreme authority naturally flow from him being our loving Creator?

6. How do the three attributes described demonstrate both God's love for his people AND his authoritative position over them? Why is it important to see both of these themes together?

SURVEY

Survey three people.

ASK: Do you believe in God? If yes, describe God. If no, why not?

If they say, "Yes," listen carefully to their response. Does it resemble the way God introduces himself or are they describing a god of their own making?

The majority of the time, when people say no, they have a reason. This is different than if you asked someone if they believe in garden fairies. In thinking about God, people can usually point to some way in which they are proactively choosing not to believe in him. Start by *listening to their answer* and seeing if anything they say pulls you back to what you learned in Genesis 1–3.

RESPONSE FROM PERSON #1:

RESPONSE FROM PERSON #2:

RESPONSE FROM PERSON #3:

NOTE FOR YOURSELF: What did you learn from your survey? What connections do you see between the survey responses and the article or the Scriptures you've been studying?

SMALL GROUP MEETING

Meet with your group to share what you learned from the survey and discuss your workbook answers.

Session

3

HUMANITY

WHY UNDERSTANDING HUMANITY MATTERS

When the gospel comes to us, it usually begins with a mirror. Wait, a mirror? You see, few people need to be convinced that the world just isn't the way it ought to be. But when pressed for answers, almost universally people point to someone else as the culprits. *It is those bigots, or those liberals, or those conservatives, or those haters, or those . . .* (we could do this all day). There's always someone to blame.

But the gospel doesn't start with those bad people out there. The gospel holds a mirror up to each one of us and forces us to reckon with what is actually true. *We* are the bad guys. Wait, let's not hide behind the first-person plural: *I am the bad guy* (and so are you).

How well do you deal with correction? How do you respond when someone calls you out? We have to prepare to humbly let God point us to the mirror and show us what is absolutely true. As you read the selection from the book of Romans this week, be prepared for a reality check.

The bad news you must acknowledge about yourself will make the good news of the gospel all the sweeter. In fact, if you try to jump ahead to the good news without first facing the bad news, you may not find the good news very compelling.

In preparing to study session 3 on humanity, we would all do well to follow the example of the famed philosopher and author G. K. Chesterton. He famously answered a newspaper's open question, *What's wrong with the world today?* by writing a very short letter to the editor.

> "Dear Sir,
> I am.
> Yours, G. K. Chesterton."

***

To prepare for your small group meeting:

- Complete the reading assignment
- Read the article
- Answer the workbook questions
- Survey three people

READING ASSIGNMENT

Read Romans 1:18–3:20 a minimum of three times. Use a different translation each time. Record your observations below.

- What does this text tell me about God?

- What does this text tell me about humanity?

Session

ARTICLE

3

As Paul sat down to write a letter to a group of Christians in Rome, he didn't want to take anything for granted in their understanding of the gospel—so he started from the very beginning! The opening chapters of Romans teach us that people instinctively know some important things about God that have been clearly seen since the creation of the world (1:20).

Along with understanding God, Paul wants us to understand *us*. Romans 1–3 give us the opportunity to look into a mirror and see some things we wish were not there. We will break down the gospel's analysis of humanity using three categories that we discover in these chapters.

HUMANITY IS WILLFULLY IGNORANT

As "modern" men and women, we bristle at categories like these. *How dare you say I'm ignorant!* However, Romans 1:18 tells us our natural response to what can be known about God is to be "people who by their unrighteousness suppress the truth." Do you see how the word *suppress* is in the present tense? Humans are in a continual, intentional state of suppressing the truth. We hold it back and push it away.

That's why describing people as ignorant of God needs a qualifier. Romans 1 teaches us that we are *willfully* ignorant. Look at the mounting descriptions Paul throws down just so that we don't miss this point: "What can be known about God *is evident among them*, because God has shown it to them. For his invisible attributes, that is, his eternal power and divine nature, have been *clearly seen* since the creation of the world, being understood through what he has made. As a result, people are *without excuse*. For though *they knew God*, they did not glorify him as God or show gratitude. Instead, their thinking became worthless, and their senseless hearts were darkened" (Romans 1:19–21, emphasis added). *WE TEND TO AVOID — NOT CONFRONT — THE TRUTH.*

We know things about God because we bear God's image. Yet our knowledge of God is distorted knowledge because of sin, and that sin has put a huge separation between us and God. It is like we are looking through a broken lens. Though we can see something recognizable, it is impossible to get a clear or full picture. Our view of God has been vandalized by our sin.

Even before I knew God as my Lord and Savior, I knew he was there, but I just avoided thinking about this so I could keep outrunning the guilt of my sin. I wanted to keep doing things my way. I knew if I stopped to think about God's true role, it would be crystal clear I was in the wrong!

Yet we are all bombarded with an undeniable message about the Creator. As Psalm 19 puts it, *GENERAL REVELATION*

> The heavens declare the glory of God,
> and the expanse proclaims the work of his hands.
> Day after day they pour out speech;
> night after night they communicate knowledge.
> There is no speech; there are no words;
> their voice is not heard.
> Their message has gone out to the whole earth,
> and their words to the ends of the world. (Psalm 19:1–4)

The testimony of creation sets in us an intuitive knowledge that there is a higher power to which we are accountable. Think about your own life. Where have you chosen to walk down a wrong path knowing full well it was wrong? Where in your life have you operated without giving a thought to how that decision honors the God of the universe?

Look at those questions again. We are all guilty of living as if God were not there. Parents, sometimes when your children disobey, you go straight to an angry response rather than patient correction. Spouses, you have made timelines and job changes and huge decisions without stopping to consider how these glorify your Maker. Students, you have unique relationships and opportunities in this time of your life, but you often give attention instead to things of little importance. *This* is a portrait of our willful ignorance.

GOD		HUMANITY
Loving Creator	→	Willfully ignorant

HUMANITY IS PASSIONATELY REBELLIOUS

Earlier we learned that God is the supreme authority over all creation. What is humanity's response to his ultimate authority? Do we gladly surrender ourselves to him, believing that our Creator is kind, generous, and worth obeying?

Not according to Romans 1–3.

Not only do we continually suppress truths God has directly revealed to us, we actively and passionately rebel against those things we intuitively know he commands. The same way Adam and Eve rebelled against the one command God gave them in the garden, we rebel against the few things we know in our gut we should obey.

It starts with refusing to acknowledge that God is supreme. We don't treat God as honorable and magnificent. We refuse to give him thanks for giving us life and breath and everything else (see Acts 17:25). Recall that we were intended to be God's *viceroys*—flourishing in an earth he

SIN MAKES US SOMETHING LESS THAN WE ARE. IT REDUCES US TO LESS. IT DEVALUES.

GOSPEL 101

created for his glory and our greatest pleasure. Yet, rather than worshiping the God who created us, we turn and worship almost everything but him. John Calvin said it aptly: "Man's nature, so to speak, is a perpetual factory of idols."[3]

Some of us show our idolatry by engaging in rampant unrighteousness. Romans 1 presents a laundry list—sexual sin, greed, envy, quarrels, malice, gossip, and much more. We have all "been there" with these sins. Some of us are still there.

But others of us demonstrate our idolatry in an equally foolish fashion. Rather than *rampant unrighteousness*, we rebel against God by living a life of *self-righteousness*. Paul says we are judgmental. "Therefore, every one of you who judges is without excuse. For when you judge another, you condemn yourself, since you, the judge, do the same things. We know that God's judgment on those who do such things is based on the truth. Do you really think—anyone of you who judges those who do such things yet do the same—that you will escape God's judgment? (Romans 2:1–3). Then Paul condemns the idea that in ourselves we can be good enough for God. "For no one will be justified in his sight by the works of the law" (Romans 3:20).

We cannot afford to miss this. There are two ways to be lost! No amount of church attendance, good deeds, or moral behavior can lessen our dependence on God. As Timothy Keller puts it, "Nearly everyone defines sin as breaking a list of rules. Jesus, though, shows us that a man who has violated virtually nothing on the list of moral misbehaviors can be every bit as spiritually lost as the most profligate, immoral person. Why? Because sin is not just breaking the rules, it is putting yourself in the place of God as Savior, Lord, and Judge. . . . There are two ways to be your own Savior and Lord. One is breaking all the moral laws and setting your own course, and one is by keeping all the moral laws and being very, very good."[4]

HOW DOES BEING GOOD MAKE YOU YOUR OWN SAVIOR? WE ARE CALLED TO OBEY?. I'M SURE KELLER IS REFERRING TO EARNING.

The common thread in our passionate rebellion is our prideful self-reliance. Paul calls us to stop justifying our evil or even our "good." If we are to stand firm in the "day of wrath, when God's righteous judgment is revealed" (Romans 2:5), *it will only be through repentance and belief in a righteousness that is not our own*—a righteousness that comes only from Jesus.

GOD		HUMANITY
Loving Creator	→	Willfully ignorant
Supreme authority	→	Passionately rebellious

HUMANITY IS CONDEMNED TO DEATH

What is the consequence of humanity's willful ignorance and passionate rebellion? Judgment before the final Judge. This is consistent with the eternal gospel we first explored in the opening pages of Genesis. God lavished his goodness on Adam and Eve, but gave them just one command: "You must not eat from the tree of the knowledge of good and evil" followed by the crystal-clear consequence, "for on the day that you eat from it, you will certainly die" (Genesis 2:17).

Yet Adam rejected God's loving authority and the Judge gave him a sentence of death. Though he did not die an immediate, physical death, he did die a *spiritual death*. He was immediately disconnected from the life-giver, being expelled from the garden and banned from the tree of life. This sentence carried with it a knowledge that physical death could come at any time. Death now hung over the heads of Adam and Eve.

Turning from Eden to ourselves, we know we have a death sentence as well. In fact, our acts of willful ignorance and passionate rebellion rumble around in our consciences precisely for this reason. We have all have sinned and fall short of God's glory. We know deep down that our self-justification of our sins is not enough. We will stand silent before the Judge, and know intuitively that his sentence is just and true.

GOD		HUMANITY
Loving Creator	→	Willfully ignorant
Supreme authority	→	Passionately rebellious
Final Judge	→	Condemned to death

APPLICATION

Based on Romans 1–3, we can define the sin of humanity as:

> My rejection of the knowledge of God and his authority over me as my Creator, as evidenced by my willful ignorance of him and my passionate rebellion against his commands

As you consider this section with your small group, reflect on what you learned about God's character from Genesis and what you learned about humanity above. Don't let this be a theoretical reflection either. Consider specific sins in your life and the specific ways God is the only solution to your lostness. Flee as far as you can from suppressing the truth about yourself and your Creator.

Romans 2:4 says God is full of kindness, restraint, and patience. Though totally justified in his sentencing, this final Judge has chosen to offer us a way to enter that judgment day without fear. How might you be able to help friends or neighbors consider their posture before God? How might you point them to their (and your) need for Jesus?

1. Think back to the big questions all humans ask themselves: Why are we here, what is wrong with the world, and what will put things right? How did you answer these questions before you knew Christ? How do you answer them now?

2. Based on Romans 1:16–3:20, list three key ways we can understand the sinfulness of humanity.

3. Read Ephesians 4:17–19. How does this further explain what you've learned about humanity?

Fill in the chart.

GOD		HUMANITY
	→	
	→	
	→	

4. What are the two ways for a person to be lost? For each of these paths, what would be the profile of someone who is lost on that path? How do they look or act? Which of these categories do you most identify with? (Read Romans 10:1–4 for further understanding on the self-righteous path of being lost.)

SURVEY

Survey three people.

ASK: On a scale of one to ten, one being completely evil and ten being completely good, how would you rate people in general?

FOLLOW UP: Why did you give this rating?

FOLLOW UP: Is there such a thing as "sin"? If so, what is it?

You will likely get a spectrum of responses to this question. One thing to keep in mind: there is no "right" answer you are looking for. Instead, their answer on this spectrum will be a gateway to hear about their view of humankind.

LISTEN to their answer. Do they rate humanity low because they have a low view of self and a high view of God? Or is it low because they see humanity as having no hope at all? Do they rate humanity high because they see the human race on a positive trajectory throughout human civilization (*We don't need God; we have this covered.*)?

RESPONSE FROM PERSON #1:

RESPONSE FROM PERSON #2:

RESPONSE FROM PERSON #3:

NOTE FOR YOURSELF: What did you learn from your survey? What connections do you see between the survey responses and the article or the Scriptures you've been studying?

SMALL GROUP MEETING

Meet with your group to share what you learned from the survey and discuss your workbook answers.

Session

4

CHRIST

WHY THE CENTRALITY OF CHRIST MATTERS

Jesus Christ is nearly universally familiar. But what do most people think of Jesus? Many (perhaps most) would say they admire Jesus. They might describe Jesus as a great teacher, as a peacemaker, maybe as an example worth following.

Unfortunately, most people have constructed a version of Jesus that barely resembles reality. Some are even bold enough to say, "To me, Jesus is _____" as if Jesus's identity is up for grabs.

So, who is Jesus and what is his role in the gospel? Is he the dying, emaciated man we see impaled on a cross? Is he the perfectly coiffed guy who looks like he came off the cover of GQ? Is he the dude in the long gown and glowing halo gently knocking on the door of your heart? No wonder people are confused about the identity of Jesus Christ—there are a lot of versions of him floating around. We need to discover the real Jesus and let him speak for himself.

More, we need to ponder how Jesus is more than a historical figure, now long past. Christians don't simply remember Jesus and rehearse his teachings. Christians are impacted daily by the life-giving power of the risen Christ.

In considering the eternal gospel, we began by meeting God and then saw how his first people rejected him and brought sin into his world. Many people stop the story there. They agree the world is corrupt, and they are cynical about it. They have given up on themselves—*I can't change who I am*. And they have given up on finding a hero who is so good he resists all corruption and instead destroys it forever.

Satan would like you to stop the story before you get to the hero, too. Maybe you have given in to a certain sin so often that you've stopped fighting it. Maybe you have sinned in a way that fills you with shame. But our story is not over! You belong to Jesus, and it is time now to see how he has beaten Satan and sin.

∗∗∗

To prepare for your small group meeting:

- Complete the reading assignment
- Read the article
- Answer the workbook questions
- Survey three people

READING ASSIGNMENT

Read 1 Corinthians 15:1–28 a minimum of three times. Use a different translation each time.

- Based on this passage, what is the gospel?

- According to this passage, why did Jesus have to die?

- What proofs or evidences does this passage offer to show that Jesus has been raised from the dead?

- Why is the resurrection of Jesus Christ of central importance to the Christian?

IT'S NOT MERELY WHAT CHRIST DOES, BUT WHO HE IS THAT MAKES WHAT HE DOES SO PROFOUND.

Session

4

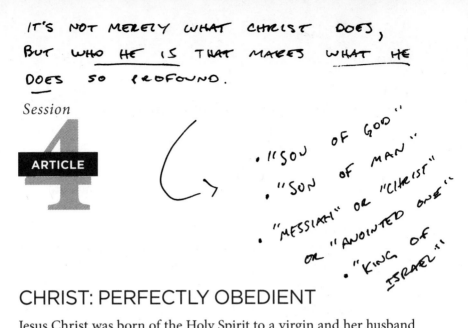

- "SON OF GOD"
- "SON OF MAN"
- "MESSIAH" OR "CHRIST" OR "ANOINTED ONE"
- "KING OF ISRAEL"

CHRIST: PERFECTLY OBEDIENT

Jesus Christ was born of the Holy Spirit to a virgin and her husband in the small village of Bethlehem. After an initial burst of divine activity—think wise men, guiding stars, and shepherds seeing angels in the sky—Jesus lived in relative obscurity as the son of a carpenter for about thirty years.

Then we see Jesus in the Jordan River being baptized. This incredible moment captures God the Father proclaiming, "This is my Son!" and the Holy Spirit descending on Jesus. How captivating this event must have been! Finally, the rescue plan to save God's image-bearers was underway!

But all of a sudden, Satan crashed the scene.

> Then Jesus was led up by the Spirit into the wilderness to be tempted by the devil. After he had fasted forty days and forty nights, he was hungry. Then the tempter approached him and said, "If you are the Son of God, tell these stones to become bread."
>
> He answered, "It is written: 'Man must not live on bread alone but on every word that comes from the mouth of God.'"
>
> Then the devil took him to the holy city, had him stand on the pinnacle of the temple, and said to him, "If you are the Son of God, throw yourself down. For it is written:

He will give his angels orders concerning you,
and they will support you with their hands
so that you will not strike
your foot against a stone."

Jesus told him, "It is also written: 'Do not test the Lord your God.'"

Again, the devil took him to a very high mountain and showed him all the kingdoms of the world and their splendor. And he said to him, "I will give you all these things if you will fall down and worship me."

Then Jesus told him, "Go away, Satan! For it is written: 'Worship the Lord your God, and serve only him.'"

Then the devil left him, and angels came and began to serve him. (Matthew 4:1–11)

Put this scene together with what you recall from the very beginning. The appearance of Satan in Matthew 4 is a clue to stop and remember the garden in the first chapters of Genesis. There, in his curse, God promised a future offspring of Eve who would crush Satan's head. Thousands of years later, there in the Jordan River, it is as if God is saying, "Oh, Satan, by the way, *here he is!*" It is no wonder Satan found his way to Jesus so fast—the snake crusher had arrived![5]

There are several remarkable similarities between Jesus's temptation and that of Adam and Eve. Just as before, Satan offers food as a temptation. Just as before, Satan twists God's words to introduce doubt. Just as before, Satan promises *you can be like God.*

Yet there are also major differences in the desert scene. In the garden, there was lushness and plenty. Adam could have anything he wanted save for the fruit of one tree. In the desert, there was nothing—Jesus was very hungry. In the garden, Adam was tempted with a vague promise that he could be like God. Whisked from the desert, Jesus could physically see the specific kingdoms that could be his *immediately.* Weary from forty days of fasting, all Jesus had to do was take a knee and he could finally eat. He could stop his suffering, prevent any future suffering, and take a shortcut to his kingdom.

The whole creation was made through Jesus, but he took on the nature of a peasant and now found himself starving in a desert. What confidence the Father must have had in his Son! It is as if Jesus was in a boxing ring blindfolded and hands tied behind his back. Yet Jesus stepped in and absorbed the blows. Father and Son knew exactly what they were doing—beginning to untangle the mess humanity had made.

You see, *this desert encounter represents a radical reversal of the garden.* Even with all of the odds in his favor, the first Adam effectively handed his God-given dominion over to Satan at the first sign of temptation. But in the desert, Jesus was unflinching against Satan even in his physically-weakened state. He adamantly defended God, untwisting Satan's misuse of Scripture and deploying it right back in his face. The promised dominion would indeed be his, but not yet. King Jesus first had to tend to some unfinished business.

Jesus was not born into the curse of sin, and he was not about to choose that path, even if that path was a shortcut. Sinlessness is part of Jesus's being, and the desert scene was but a snapshot of his whole life on this earth. In stark contrast to the willful ignorance of the rest of humanity, Jesus was perfectly obedient to his Father.

GOD		HUMANITY		CHRIST
Loving Creator	→	Willfully ignorant	→	Perfectly obedient

CHRIST: SUBSTITUTIONARY SACRIFICE

Yet what does Christ's perfect obedience actually mean for us? Are we to look on him and just appreciate his abilities? Is he simply a good moral example to follow?

If this were the case, we would still be left without an answer to our sin problem. Even with Jesus being all-good, we are still passionately rebellious and would continue to subvert God's supreme authority just like we have always done. A worthy model is not enough.

By God's grace, Jesus is far more than a good example to follow. Rather, "He made the one who did not know sin to be sin for us, so that in him we might become the righteousness of God" (2 Corinthians 5:21).

This one verse aptly summarizes what theologians call the Great Exchange. As with any exchange, each party comes together and receives something from the other. As people who believe in Jesus, what do we get from him? The righteousness of God. And what does Jesus get from us? Our sin.

This concept of substitution is not a new idea to the New Testament; it is woven through the entire Bible. A great example is found in Isaiah 53.

> Yet he himself bore our sicknesses,
> and he carried our pains;
> but we in turn regarded him stricken,
> struck down by God, and afflicted.
> But he was pierced because of our rebellion,
> crushed because of our iniquities;
> punishment for our peace was on him,
> and we are healed by his wounds.
> We all went astray like sheep;
> we all have turned to our own way;
> and the LORD has punished him
> for the iniquity of us all.
>
> He was oppressed and afflicted,
> yet he did not open his mouth.
> Like a lamb led to the slaughter
> and like a sheep silent before her shearers,
> he did not open his mouth.

He was taken away because of oppression and judgment;
and who considered his fate?
For he was cut off from the land of the living;
he was struck because of my people's rebellion.
(Isaiah 53:4–8)

How is humanity described here? Sick. Pained. Laden with iniquity.
As lost sheep.

Human beings are anemic and powerless. Sin has latched its taproot
into our souls and drained the life breathed into us by God. Like sheep,
we are, to put it bluntly, dumb and constantly going astray. Without the
shepherd, we are vulnerable, weak, and prone to wander.

And then, in a shocking change of the analogy, Isaiah ascribes the sheep
metaphor to Jesus! Taking the form of one of these sheep, it is not us
led to slaughter, but Christ! On our way to the slaughterhouse, Jesus
interrupts our death march. He bore our sicknesses, he was punished,
he carried our pain, and earned us peace.

Again, Jesus was not just a good example. He is not just a good model
of morality for us to follow. This sin—this terrible darkness that has
caused murder and death and depression and evil—yes, this sin that
has been at fault for every single tear ever cried—he *became* this sin for
us when he gave himself to be killed on the cross.

GOD		HUMANITY		CHRIST
Loving Creator	→	Willfully ignorant	→	Perfectly obedient
Supreme authority	→	Passionately rebellious	→	Substitutionary sacrifice

CHRIST: VICTORIOUSLY RISEN

Yet if Christ's work ended with his death, how terrible that would be!

If Christ himself could not defeat death, then that which killed him would still be there, lingering. Satan would be crouching at the door in wait for us, just as he had been since the time of Adam (see Genesis 4:7). Our situation would not be all that different!

Romans 6:4–5 tells us, "Therefore we were buried with him by baptism into death, in order that, just as Christ was raised from the dead by the glory of the Father, so we too may walk in newness of life. For if we have been united with him in the likeness of his death, we will certainly also be in the likeness of his resurrection."

Sin held a rightful claim on humanity: death. Our willing and passionate participation with sin against the final Judge left us condemned to die. To require anything less than perfect obedience would infer that sin itself was not all that bad. Remember the lie in the garden? *Surely God won't punish you.* I shudder just imagining that serpent and his voice!

The victorious resurrection of Christ certainly ensures our future victory over the grave. But it does far more. Much of the New Testament is dedicated to helping Christ-followers live daily in the power of resurrection life. For instance, Romans 6 teaches us that we can finally say no to sin and yes to righteousness. We are no longer slaves to sin! Colossians 3 teaches me how to "put off" my old way of life and "put on" things like compassion, kindness, and humility. The book of 1 Peter teaches me how suffering can actually become a source of joy in my life. And that's just scratching the surface. There are layers upon layers of benefits that come to us every day because of the resurrection of Jesus Christ. WHAT ARE THOSE BENEFITS?

Where our sin sentenced us to being condemned to death before our final Judge, Christ took our punishment and was victoriously raised from the grave. And that victory is ours to live in every single day, culminating in our victory over the grave. He is truly the offspring from Eve that could crush Satan and bring us freedom!

IF I'M A SLAVE TO CHRIST, I'M FREE. IF I'M FREE FROM CHRIST, I'M A SLAVE TO SIN.

GOD		HUMANITY		CHRIST
Loving Creator	→	Willfully ignorant	→	Perfectly obedient
Supreme authority	→	Passionately rebellious	→	Substitutionary sacrifice
Final Judge	→	Condemned to death	→	Victoriously risen

APPLICATION

Throughout this resource, I have been taking you to both the beginning and the end of Scripture as we discuss the gospel message. Similarly, in 1 Corinthians 15, Paul expertly connects Christ's life, death, and resurrection to Genesis and Revelation. From the start of creation, God had a plan to take corruptible people and make them incorruptible.

The gospel message is not *Jesus died to forgive my sins and now I'm going to just meddle around until it's time to go to heaven.* No, Jesus descended from his heavenly status, lived a perfect life, *became* sin for us, died to take our deserved punishment, and rose again so we could be freed from our death sentence and live as the "righteousness of God in him." We are no longer slaves to sin, but are unified with this Christ. *We are in him and he is in us.*

At home, in the workplace, and in the classroom, we can live once again live under the kingdom of God. In Christ, we are once again God's viceroys! With this in mind, how can you execute his will and demonstrate his love on this earth today?

Session

WORKBOOK

1. Complete the chart.

GOD		HUMANITY		CHRIST
_____	→	_____	→	_____
_____	→	_____	→	_____
_____	→	_____	→	_____

2. How is the temptation of Jesus Christ similar to the temptation of Adam and Eve? How is it different? Why is this important?

3. What do we receive from Jesus through his sacrifice on the cross?

4. Why is the resurrection of Jesus Christ of central importance to the Christian? In writing your answer, refer to 1 Corinthians 15, Ephesians 2:4–10, and Romans 8:8–11.

5. How did Jesus's work change your life upon your salvation? How does being united with Christ change your everyday life?

SURVEY

Survey three people.

ASK: Who is Jesus?

Once again, my main suggestion here is to be a LISTENER and guide your conversation based on the person's unique answer. Check yourself constantly to make sure your goal in these conversations is not to play a comparison game between your faith journey and someone else's. Be a humble servant.

Some will say Jesus is their Lord and Savior. Dig into that a bit. Ask if they would consider themselves a devoted Christ-follower. How would their life be different if Christ were not a part of their life?

Some will say Jesus was a historical figure but is not the Son of God. Or they will say Jesus may be the answer for some people but not for them. Ask them why they believe this—what is their evidence or backstory? Ask what it would take for them to believe Jesus is the Son of God. Consider pointing them to what you learned about God and about humanity in order to illustrate how everyone needs Jesus Christ.

RESPONSE FROM PERSON #1:

RESPONSE FROM PERSON #2:

RESPONSE FROM PERSON #3:

NOTE FOR YOURSELF: What did you learn from your survey? What connections do you see between the survey responses and the article or the Scriptures you've been studying?

SMALL GROUP MEETING

Meet with your group to share what you learned from the survey and discuss your workbook answers.

Session

5

JUSTIFICATION

WHY JUSTIFICATION MATTERS

The biblical concept of *justification* is at the heart of the eternal gospel and is of utmost importance to the believer. It is perhaps the best lens to gain a clear picture of how Christ's work impacts our salvation. There are many common misunderstandings about this work of Christ, so it is important to stop and consider justification as we seek to share his gospel with others.

Some people resent Christians because they think Christians claim to have a leg up on others in being right and good. *You think you're better, huh?* But what if Christ-followers actually claim zero credit for being right in God's eyes? What if, of all people, they actually can be most comfortable saying *I was wrong* because their rightness doesn't depend on themselves?

It is also true that there are Christians who tend to be burdened continually by trying to be good enough for God. They are constantly under a cloud of guilt and shame. This is a miserable way to walk through life and can eventually drive people to despair, bitterness, and anger at themselves, at others, at God—or all the above!

Justification means we are made right in God's eyes. It is central to the message of the gospel and it is central to the way Christians are to walk in the newness of life that the gospel promises. Ask God to open your mind and heart to a fresh awareness of the beauty of justification.

* * *

To prepare for your small group meeting:

- Complete the reading assignment
- Read the article
- Answer the workbook questions
- Survey three people

READING ASSIGNMENT

Read Romans 3:19–4:25 a minimum of three times. Use a different translation each time.

- Note how often the following terms appear:

  Law

  Grace

  Faith

  Righteous/Righteousness

- In two or three sentences, describe what you can learn about each of these terms just from this reading:

  Law

  Grace

Faith

Righteous/Righteousness

ARTICLE

In conversation, the word *justification* usually comes up only when referring to an explanation for someone's behavior. In my experience, this word tends to come with a negative connotation: *Sam came up with every excuse in the book to justify his need for control.*

The biblical understanding of justification is far richer, and it holds eternal consequences for us all! It is about no longer being guilty in God's eyes and receiving punishment, but instead being counted righteous and receiving life. Let's start our understanding of justification by zooming in on four points made in the third chapter of Romans.

1. "No one will be justified in his sight by the works of the law" (Romans 3:20). Every human being stands guilty before God, the final Judge. Picturing ourselves before the judge's bench, you and I and every human can only stand silently, waiting, knowing we are guilty.

2. "But now, apart from the law, a righteousness of God has been revealed" (v. 21). *But now.* In my Bible, I have some heavy underlines beneath those words! *But now* God steps in. He reveals a source of righteousness that is outside of any good works we do. It is the righteousness of God for all who believe in Jesus.

3. "They are justified freely by his grace" (v. 24). God declares us innocent even though we don't deserve that righteousness. Instead of earning it, God brings it to us.

4. "A person is justified by faith" (v. 28). In case we missed the point, Paul circles back to clarify. We *receive* justification by faith apart from good works we do. Jesus does the justifying, and we merely receive it as we trust him.

Based on our biblical understanding, then, we can land on an operational definition of justification. Wayne Grudem defines it this way: "Justification is an instantaneous legal act of God in which he (1) thinks of our sins as forgiven and thinks of Christ's righteousness as belonging to us, and (2) declares us to be righteous in His sight."[6]

This is a good, concise understanding, and we can nod along with this definition. But where would the fun be in that? If we dig further, there are some amazing truths to mediate on.

JUSTIFICATION: WE ARE MORE THAN JUST INNOCENT

Imagine yourself standing before a judge, waiting to be sentenced to death for a crime you committed. As the verdict is announced and you are declared guilty, something shocking happens. The judge rises from his place, walks out to where you are seated, and tells the bailiff to release you. As you stand free, in shock, you watch as the judge himself is placed in your chains, taking your punishment and penalty. You are set free because of the *substitution* of the judge on your behalf.

Now, one could give this analogy and stop there. Yet justification, in the way the Bible speaks of it, is much better still.

Beyond taking your guilt, imagine the judge then leans over to you and hands you his keys, saying, "I want you to possess all that I own. My car, my house, my bank account—it's all yours."

This is justification. Jesus took the punishment for our sin when he died on the cross to set you free from the penalty of your sins AND give you the very righteousness and perfection of Jesus!

One of my favorite theologians, R. C. Sproul, created a great visual for understanding this aspect of justification: the three circles.[7] Below, you will see three empty circles. In the circle on the left, just color in or shade that circle until it is filled. This is a picture of us in guilt. We are full of darkness and death, saturated in sin. The first part of justification clears out this sin and leaves us innocent. In accordance with this, leave the middle circle totally white. Then, in the third circle, draw in some plus signs (be generous!). This is where we get the full picture of justification. Not only was the sin removed from us, but the righteousness of Jesus is credited to our account!

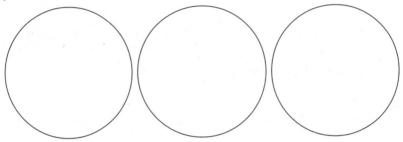

HOW DO WE RECEIVE JUSTIFICATION?

So, justification is God declaring us innocent *and* Christ giving us his righteousness. But how do we receive this justification? On this question, Scripture is clear: by faith alone.

"Because we know that a person is not justified by the works of the law but by faith in Jesus Christ, even we ourselves have believed in Christ Jesus so that we might be justified by faith in Christ and not by the works of the law, because by the works of the law no human being will be justified" (Galatians 2:16).

"For you are saved by grace through faith, and this is not from yourselves; it is God's gift—not from works, so that no one can boast" (Ephesians 2:8–9).

Justification comes as a result of God's grace—a free gift—which means we don't deserve it nor can we earn it. Justification also comes to us *by faith*, which means we trust God to do for us what we cannot do for ourselves.

Yet followers of Jesus *are* committed to obey God and do good works, and believers have sometimes been confused about the roles of faith and good works. To gain appreciation for how justification *does* work in our lives, it helps to look at some misunderstandings about how we receive justification.

FOUR FALSE VIEWS OF JUSTIFICATION[8]

False view #1: Good Works = Justification

The false claim: God looks down and sees that my good deeds outweigh my bad deeds, so I can be justified apart from faith.

The response: If works could earn us justification, why did Jesus have to come at all? This view totally removes the wonder of the cross!

False view #2: Faith + Good Works = Justification

The false claim: Through my good works (or through religious good works such as baptism, church attendance, or penance), justification can be administered to me through my church. *Faith is a necessary condition for justification, but it is not sufficient.* My good works are still required.

The response: *Only* faith in Christ and *his* righteousness brings justification (as we can see in Romans 5:1, Galatians 2:16, and Ephesians 2:8–9). To say that my good works are also necessary means the grounds of my salvation lie somehow in my own righteousness rather than Christ's!

False view #3: Profession of Faith = Justification

The false claim: I made a profession of faith in Christ at one time in my life. Because of this, good works can be totally absent from my life.

The response: Ephesians 2:8–9 is a great passage describing justification by faith alone. If this verse stood by itself, one could argue that this claim is plausible. Yet look at the very next verse. "For we are his workmanship, created in Christ Jesus for good works, which God prepared ahead of time for us to do" (Ephesians 2:10). Yes, justification is by faith alone. But good works will also emerge in your life as a result of God's work!

False view #4: Faith = Justification, but Good Works = Right Standing Before God

The false claim: Yes, faith is necessary and sufficient for justification, but I also need to do good works in order to maintain my acceptance by God. I have to keep working to make sure he continues to love me and justify me.

The response: This claim is the essence of legalism—seeking to achieve forgiveness from God and acceptance by God through obedience to God.[9] But the mistake legalists make comes in basing the reality of their *justification* on the progress they are making in *sanctification* (holy living). This is another way of trying to do on your own what only God can do!

In opposition to these views, we must hold firm that it is Christ alone who provides all the work and the righteousness necessary for justification. But when this happens, our faith in the finished work of Jesus is also demonstrated by our works. God sets us free! We live in the light! We are so changed by him that good works will emerge in our lives.

It is a huge comfort to know our justification depends on Jesus, not on how good we are. What a relief! And it is sweet encouragement to also know we begin, already in this life, to act like our Savior.

THE PROBLEM OF JUSTIFICATION

Okay, so all of this is well and good, but we are still missing something. If we accept all that we have learned about God in this study—his supreme authority, judgment, and holiness—we have to ask how a God of justice can give this beautiful gift to a sinful people.

To answer that question, a story . . .

The Merciful King[10]

Once upon a time in a kingdom far away, there lived a great king. He was simultaneously the most powerful man in the kingdom and the kindest and gentlest man in the entire realm. The kingdom was known for its peace, harmony, and goodwill. Neighbors cherished one another and years would pass without a single crime being committed. One day, however, the chief servant of the merciful king came into the throne room with ill tidings. "There is a thief in the realm of your kingdom, sire," said the servant. The king was astonished! "Find that thief! And when you do, bring him to me. He will be punished with ten lashes!" Those in the room were astonished. It had been so long since a crime had been committed that they could hardly imagine who would have done such a thing.

A week went by and the servant again made his way into the throne room. "I have bad news for you, sire," the servant reported quietly. "The thief has not been found and he continues to rob from your people." In anger, the king raised his voice and said, "Find the thief and when you do he will receive twenty-five lashes!" The people began to murmur among themselves, "Who could withstand such a punishment? Who could possibly be committing such a crime?" But as time went on, the servant once again came back into the throne room with yet another bad report. "Your Majesty, the thief has not been found. We have searched in vain for him. Your people are still being robbed." The king was enraged. "Find that wretched thief! And when you do his punishment will be fifty lashes!" Now the people were filled with dread. They were not even sure the king himself could withstand such a punishment. And if he could not, then certainly no one could. Who could be doing such a thing?

Soon afterward, the servant again approached the king in his throne room. His face was pale and his voice timid and hollow. "Your Highness," spoke the servant, "the thief has been found." "Bring him to me this instant!" cried the king. The crowd that had poured into the throne room slowly parted revealing the thief who now stood trembling in the middle of the room. To the utter shock and dismay of all, it was the king's aged mother.

There she stood, trembling and crying. Her small and frail body was shaking with fear and shame. She was, perhaps, the very last soul that anyone would have suspected of such a crime. And there stood the king, deeply wounded. The crowd began to wonder and murmur among themselves. What will the merciful king do? Will he set aside the law and display his love and mercy by forgiving his mother for her crimes? Or will he display his sovereignty and justice by giving her exactly what she deserves? Will he choose mercy or will he choose justice?

The king raised his hand to quiet the crowd. "Bring the whipping post," he said. The crowd was dumbfounded. Would the king truly have his mother receive such a punishment? Even the king could scarcely survive such a flogging! This frail woman would not last even a few strokes. The old woman was tied to the post. Her garment was rent, exposing her back to the whip-master. Her ribs could be counted for her frailty. "Administer the lashes," said the king. Not a sound could be heard as the whip was raised.

But just as the whip master was about to unleash his first stroke, the king cried, "Halt!" The crowd sighed in utter relief! But not for long. The king stood from his throne. He slowly removed the crown from his head, laying it upon the regal seat. As he began to walk down the stairs toward his mother, he laid aside his royal robe and finely woven tunic. Coming to his mother, he wrapped his enormous body around her, completely enveloping her under his frame. "Now, administer the lashes," said the king.

In this story, we see the king display pure mercy and perfect justice, "so as to be just and the one who justifies those who have faith in Jesus" (Romans 3:26 NIV).

For all the technical terms we could discuss, for all the shapes we could draw or false understandings we could dissect, there is nothing quite like a story to fix our eyes on the work of our Savior!

APPLICATION

Hopefully, through this chapter you have seen elements of this topic of justification that align with your own salvation experience. I also hope that reflecting on Christ's role in justification has driven you to love God more! But, what does it mean in our daily lives?

First, this understanding will ease the burden of works in your relationship with Christ. In our relationships, we as humans have a way of piling on misunderstandings and expectations that slowly separate us from what is most true. *Why did he do that? Does she really think that about me?* The same thing happens in our relationship with Christ. We are often so burdened by the prospect of doing enough good to be accepted by Christ. In your small group, you will be able to discuss some of the ways a true understanding of justification should impact your life experience.

Also, understanding justification will help you pull others away from false conceptions of justification as you evangelize and disciple people. Look again at the four false views of justification. Each of these hovers close to the truth but holds implications that are opposite of the gospel. With your new understanding, you can keep people from these false views from the very start.

Session

WORKBOOK

1. In one or two sentences, define justification.

2. We are more than just innocent. Why is it important to clarify this aspect of justification?

3. How do we receive justification?

4. Which of the four false views of justification have you seen in your life experience? How did you see them expressed? Why does it matter if someone holds a false view on this topic?

5. How should the truth about justification transform us?

6. How does understanding justification shape how you will share the gospel with others?

SURVEY

Survey three people.

ASK: Is there more than one way to God? Please explain.

In this question, you will gather some perspective on what is called the exclusivity of Christ. In the biblical view, Christ is *the* way, *the* truth, and *the* life, and no one comes to the Father except through him (John 14:6). However, many believe there are multiple ways to God.

Your first task, as usual, will be to LISTEN. It is truly fascinating what people believe about this question. Try to get to the evidence and back-story—why do they believe this? Do they have a distinct source? Or is it a hodgepodge of different ideas?

A helpful word picture is that of a mountain.[11] Ask if their view is that God is on top of the mountain and that different people have different paths they could take to get there? If they agree with this summary, then you can ask, "What if I told you God came down from the mountain to his people?" From here, you have a great opportunity to describe the work of Christ.

RESPONSE FROM PERSON #1:

RESPONSE FROM PERSON #2:

RESPONSE FROM PERSON #3:

NOTE FOR YOURSELF: What did you learn from your survey? What connections do you see between the survey responses and the article or the Scriptures you've been studying?

SMALL GROUP MEETING

Meet with your group to share what you learned from the survey and discuss your workbook answers.

Session

6

"THE GOSPEL DEMANDS A RESPONSE."

RESPONSE

WHY OUR RESPONSE MATTERS

So far in our study, we have focused on the content of the gospel message. But it is also imperative to explore the proper response to the gospel. In looking at Scripture, we see the example of people *understanding* the gospel and then *responding* with repentance, belief, and baptism.

Consider your own life for a moment. Think of the most hurtful sin you've ever committed. It's painful to think about, but actually take a minute and think about it—even write it down somewhere.

Genuine Christians don't pretend to be sinless. We are more aware of our sins than ever before. The difference is that we know what to do with sin. It doesn't have to haunt us, to strangle us. The gospel teaches us how to respond to sin.

In thinking about this, we see the wonder of the gospel response. By repenting, you can turn away from that sin and be a new person. By faith in Jesus, you are eternally forgiven from that sin. What joy to leave your sin and shame behind! This is what happens when you respond to Jesus.

That sin you wrote down? You can tear it up and leave it behind. The gospel teaches us how.

To put it simply, when we encounter the gospel message, we respond. We are not those who proclaim something that has had no inward effect. Instead, we gleefully pass to Jesus the sins and burdens that have weighed us down! When we hear the gospel message, we immediately forsake our old ways and trust in Christ to lead us from that point forward.

* * *

To prepare for your small group meeting:

- Complete the reading assignment
- Read the article
- Answer the workbook questions
- Survey three people

READING ASSIGNMENT

Read through Acts 17:16–34 a minimum of three times. Use a different translation each time if possible.

NOTE: Early in your reading you will encounter a reference to two groups of philosophers that were in the audience listening to Paul. Because we don't usually run into these guys when we are in the produce aisle or the gas station, let me give you a little background. Epicurean philosophers followed the ancient philosopher Epicurus. He held that pleasure was the chief goal of life, with the pleasure being a life of tranquility free from pain, disturbing passions, superstitious fears, and anxiety about death. Epicurus did not deny the existence of God (or "gods") but was deistic, meaning he believed the gods took no interest in the lives of humans. The Stoic philosophers didn't follow a single philosopher, but a rather whole school of thought known as Stoicism. It centered on living life harmoniously with nature and emphasized

HEDONISM

man's rational abilities and individual self-sufficiency. Stoics were basically pantheistic and thought of a "world-soul" as god. Knowing a little background, see if you can see why Paul chooses his words carefully, knowing his audience.

- Outline the main ideas Paul addresses in his presentation of the gospel in Acts 17.

- What does Paul address in Acts 17 about the following key themes of the gospel that we have covered so far?
  God

  Humanity

  Christ

  Justification

Session

ARTICLE

When asked, "What is the gospel?" you could answer by describing justification and you would be spot-on. Justification is at the heart of what God has done for us in Christ. "Therefore, since we have been declared righteous by faith, we have peace with God through our Lord Jesus Christ" (Romans 5:1). Note that *declared righteous* means the same thing as *justified*, and the Greek word originally used in this verse can be translated either way.

Yet what are the implications of this gospel? How does it apply to our lives?

Think of it like this: If you are asked, "How can I get rid of this headache?" there are two equally valid answers. You could explain what happens chemically and physiologically when pain medication is ingested into the human body. Or you could say, "Here, swallow this medication and your headache will go away." The first answer focuses on how the medication works. The second answer describes how to apply it to your condition.

We want people to know what God has done for us in Christ (how the gospel works). We also want people to respond to the gospel (applying it to their condition).

In this lesson, we will explore the *response* to the gospel. And to do that we will look again to the apostle Paul. This time we will listen in as he proclaims the gospel and urges a response from the listeners. While there are several examples of gospel presentations in the book of Acts, we will focus on an encounter Paul had while visiting the city of Athens.

Notice in this scene that Paul is "telling the good news about Jesus and the resurrection" (Acts 17:18). The phrase *the good news* here is another way of saying *the gospel*. They shove him on center stage, put a mic in his hand, and sit down to hear him out.

From the Areopagus in Athens, Paul would have been looking at a scene of several impressive temples. These people were indeed "extremely religious." This is not an ancient phenomenon. Even today you could drop into almost any city around the world and see places of worship. Istanbul, Bangkok, Moscow, São Paulo, Chicago, Lusaka, Paris, and Osage, Iowa, all have something in common. They are full of extremely religious people.

Paul seemed to follow the script of Genesis 1–3 as he unpacked the eternal gospel for that religious crowd. Paul described a loving Creator who has supreme authority and is the final Judge. The descriptions of humanity and the descriptions of God are as true today as they were on that ancient hill in Athens.

And just as Paul was bringing the gospel message to a climactic presentation of Jesus, the crowd seemed to want none of it. They began to ridicule Paul, and his captive audience dispersed. But even though we don't have the last page from Paul's sermon notes, we can see where he was going and we can see the *response* he was calling for. The Creator and Judge of all the earth commands every person on his earth to repent (17:30). → Metanoeo: "TO CHANGE ONE'S MIND OR PURPOSE"

What does it mean to repent? John Stott states, "Repentance is a definite turn from every thought, word, deed and habit which is known to be wrong. It is not sufficient to feel pangs of remorse or to make some kind of apology to God. Fundamentally, repentance is a matter neither of emotion nor of speech. It is an inward change of mind and attitude toward sin which leads to a change of behavior."[12]

2 COR. 7:9-11

The command to repent and believe can be found as early as the very first sermon Jesus gave. "After John was arrested, Jesus went to Galilee, proclaiming the good news of God: 'The time is fulfilled, and the kingdom of God has come near. Repent and believe the good news!'" (Mark 1:14–15).

Repentance and belief go together like inhaling and exhaling. Both are essential to the Christian life. Repentance describes what we turn from, and belief describes what we turn toward. In *repentance* we change our minds about sin as we forsake it. In *belief* we trust solely in the finished work of Christ for the forgiveness of sins and the hope of eternal life. Again, this gospel is not just for informational purposes. It is not just a message. It is not just a story. The gospel impacts reality! *Repentance and belief are the means by which this good news is actually applied to our lives.*

The command is the same now as it was then. The call on you and on the people to whom you bring the gospel is this: repent and believe.

THE ROLE OF BAPTISM IN THE NEW TESTAMENT

In the New Testament, the response to the gospel was tangible and physical. Those who repented and believed were baptized to demonstrate outwardly that something inwardly had changed.

Look at how the apostle Paul connects believers' repentance and faith with baptism:

> Or are you unaware that all of us who were baptized into Christ Jesus were baptized into his death? Therefore we were buried with him by baptism into death, in order that, just as Christ was raised from the dead by the glory of the Father, so we too may walk in newness of life. (Romans 6:3–4)

You were also circumcised in him with a circumcision not done with hands, by putting off the body of flesh, in the circumcision of Christ, when you were buried with him in baptism, in which you were also raised with him through faith in the working of God, who raised him from the dead. And when you were dead in trespasses and in the uncircumcision of your flesh, he made you alive with him and forgave us all our trespasses. (Colossians 2:11–13)

Baptism is the outward expression that someone has embraced the gospel of Jesus Christ. It is why Jesus commissioned his followers with these words: "All authority has been given to me in heaven and on earth. Go, therefore, and make disciples of all nations, *baptizing them in the name of the Father and of the Son and of the Holy Spirit*, teaching them to observe everything I have commanded you. And remember, I am with you always, to the end of the age" (Matthew 28:18–20, emphasis added).

The core content of the gospel is justification. It is how God makes us right with him. The core response to the gospel is to repent and believe. And the outward manifestation of this internal change comes through being baptized.

"WHAT ABOUT RE-BAPTISM?"

APPLICATION

As we discussed in previous sessions, people do not want to admit they are not in control of their own destiny. We are naturally ignorant and rebellious. However, this is precisely why repentance and belief are such a powerful response in the Christian life. In a counterintuitive reversal, it is this death of self that brings true life.

Repentance is like refreshing rain. "Therefore repent and turn back, so that your sins may be wiped out, that seasons of refreshing may come from the presence of the Lord" (Acts 3:19–20).

Repentance brings a clean conscience. "For godly grief produces a repentance that leads to salvation without regret" (2 Corinthians 7:10).

This death-to-life transfer is best illustrated by the act of baptism. In this new life, we are able to lock back in step with things-as-they-should-be. We can breathe again! We are free!

As you meet with your small group, consider what your next steps may be. Who in your life is in need of refreshing that will only come through repentance? Perhaps, even, your next step is to be baptized or to encourage a new believer to be baptized.

Session

WORKBOOK

6

1. How is humanity described in Acts 17? How is God described?

2. What does Acts 17 say about Christ and justification?

3. What did you find particularly helpful about Paul's example of how to engage others in Acts 17? How does he show his knowledge of the local context and culture as he shares the gospel?

4. What is repentance? What is belief? Why do these seem to be partnered throughout the New Testament?

5. What does baptism picture? Who is to be baptized?

6. How did you respond to the gospel initially? What do repentance and belief look like in your own life?

SURVEY

Survey three people.

ASK: How will God determine who goes to heaven and who goes to hell?

This question will elicit interesting perspectives on people's view of God, heaven, hell, faith and works, and justification. Whatever the case, you will be able to LISTEN and offer both understanding and an alternate perspective.

Some people will hold onto a "balance" view: those who do more good than bad will go to heaven, and those who do more bad than good will go to hell. In this case, consider leaning on what you've learned so far about the gap between humankind and God. *All fall short of the glory of God.*

Others will lean into one aspect of God's character: God is love, surely no one will go to hell. In this case, consider what you've learned about the fullness of God's character. He is love, and he is just. Sin cannot go unpunished.

Still others will regard both heaven and hell as theoretical concepts. In this case, consider tapping back into what we learned about human beings suppressing the truth. How do they know these are theoretical concepts? What is the evidence/backstory?

RESPONSE FROM PERSON #1:

RESPONSE FROM PERSON #2:

RESPONSE FROM PERSON #3:

NOTE FOR YOURSELF: What did you learn from your survey? What connections do you see between the survey responses and the article or the Scriptures you've been studying?

SMALL GROUP MEETING

Meet with your group to share what you learned from the survey and discuss your workbook answers.

7

BELONGING

WHY BELONGING MATTERS

Once we understand the gospel and respond with repentance and belief, we are not immediately made perfect and taken up into heaven. Instead, we walk back into the same old world—a world still lost and hopeless—but as people who now belong to God and to each other. We are adopted into God's family and grow over time to be more and more like our Father.

We are not perfect, but growing. There is a whole new power at work within us. There is real and deep change occurring in our lives. We no longer need to live in utter shame because of our failures. Instead, we find forgiveness for our failures and hope for lasting change. We belong to Christ! And he is changing everything.

We are no longer orphans. On our own, we as people feel disconnected. We have shallow relationships, and we want more from our spouse or our parents or our friends. We sense that belonging should be deeper and lasting. Here is the good news: through the gospel, we have perfect, never-ending belonging to God.

We are no longer lonely. When we say yes to Christ, we are invited into community with millions of others who are orienting their lives toward their King. The wife whose husband is growing distant can find encouragement and support in her new extended family. The student who dulls away the boredom of life by watching Netflix now has new friends and a rejuvenated meaning to life. We belong to Christ and we belong to each other in the gospel.

***

To prepare for your small group meeting:

- Complete the reading assignment
- Read the article
- Answer the workbook questions
- Survey three people

READING ASSIGNMENT

Read Romans 6–8, plus chapter 12, a minimum of three times. Use a different translation each time.

- Summarize each chapter of Romans 6–8 in two or three sentences.
    Chapter 6

    Chapter 7

    Chapter 8

- Paul concludes his long treatise on the gospel with a beautiful song of worship in Romans 11:33–36. Then he turns his attention to the application of the gospel in the remaining chapters of Romans. He immediately begins to teach the Roman Christians how vital it is that they live out the gospel with one another, in community. According to Romans 12, how would you summarize Paul's admonition to be one body?

"Therefore, brothers and sisters, in view of the mercies of God, I urge you to present your bodies as a living sacrifice, holy and pleasing to God; this is your true worship. Do not be conformed to this age, but be transformed by the renewing of your mind, so that you may discern what is the good, pleasing, and perfect will of God" (Romans 12:1–2).

A NEW IDENTITY

As we read these verses, the opening word *therefore* sweeps the first eleven chapters of Romans into memory. Paul is saying, "Based on all that I have taught you about the gospel, here is what life in the gospel should look like." Though brief, Paul's instructions here are powerful. He knows how to pack a lot of instruction into a small space!

As people who have received the "mercies of God," Paul calls believers to offer our lives to God. Notice how tangible and "real" Paul is. He doesn't call on believers to give Jesus just their *hearts*. He calls them to offer their *whole bodies* to God as a living sacrifice. The gospel teaches us that we can now love the Lord our God with all our heart, with all our soul, with all our mind, and with all our strength (Mark 12:30).

God doesn't expect instant transformation, but he does call us to begin to live out our new identity. Romans 12:2 is written in present tense. The renewing of our mind will continue and grow as we seek to live in accordance with our new life.

SANCTIFICATION

This transformation and renewing of the mind is called *sanctification*. Wayne Grudem defines it this way: "Sanctification is a progressive work of God and man that makes us more and more free from sin and like Christ in our actual lives."[13]

Compare this to what we learned about justification in previous sessions. *Justification* is an instantaneous act of God on our behalf. *Sanctification* is a lifelong process. This is important to note because all believers experience a tension in their new life in Christ: *Why do I still sin?* Paul spends Romans 6 and 7 unpacking this tension for us. Coming alongside Paul's explanation, here is a helpful word picture used by D. Martyn Lloyd-Jones:[14]

> Imagine you are an emancipated slave. You are free from the tyranny of your former owner and master. You decide to start a new life as a free man. Incredibly, a farm is given to you right next to your old slave master. You begin to live your new life, yet your former slave owner continues to call you from across the fence and demand that you submit to him. You know you've been set free, but you can't seem to shake his influence. His voice may frighten you and even cause you to flinch. You may even begin to obey him.

But stop! You can turn and face your old master and, by the power of Christ, say, "No! You don't own me."

Paul summarizes it this way: "So, you too consider yourselves dead to sin but alive to God in Christ Jesus. Therefore do not let sin reign in your mortal body, so that you obey its desires. And do not offer any parts of it to sin as weapons for unrighteousness. But *as those who are alive from the dead, offer yourselves to God*, and all the parts of yourselves to God as weapons for righteousness. *For sin will not rule over you*, because you are not under law but under grace" (Romans 6:11–14, emphasis added).

Let me emphasize something here. Sanctification is incredible good news. God is not looking down on us and simply ordering us to clean up our lives. He is pouring supernatural power into our lives so we can live the kind of life we have always wanted to but could never pull off on our own! And if we ever get impatient with ourselves or frustrated with our lack of forward movement, we look up into the adoring eyes of our heavenly Father who is saying, "Remember, I love you with an everlasting love. I will never leave you. I will never forsake you. Now let me show you how to live."

The process of sanctification is all about finally having the power to turn away from your enslaved, old self and living in accordance with the new, true identity you have as one who has been saved by Christ. You will have missteps along the way, but your identity is the same. You have been adopted as a child of God.

ADOPTION

As we travel through Romans, the story continues to get better and better, and the crescendo peaks in chapter 8. We belong in God's family. We have gone from slaves to sons and daughters of God! "All those led by God's Spirit are God's sons. You did not receive a spirit of slavery to fall back into fear. Instead, you received the Spirit of adoption, by whom we cry out, "*Abba*, Father!" The Spirit himself testifies together with our spirit that we are God's children, and if children, also heirs—heirs of God and coheirs with Christ—if indeed we suffer with him so that we may also be glorified with him" (Romans 8:14–17).

Adoption is the work of God whereby he takes those who were not part of his family and he makes them his children.[15] We once lowered our eyes in shame and fear before God. Now, we lift our voices and cry out to him, "Abba, Father!" No longer is he a distant ruler we have dishonored.

God has become our Father. And this radically reshapes our identity. As J. I. Packer puts it, "Our understanding of Christianity cannot be better than our grasp of adoption. . . . If you want to judge how well a person understands Christianity, find out how much he makes of the thought of being God's child, and having God as his Father. If this is not the thought that prompts and controls his worship and prayers and whole outlook on life, it means that he does not understand Christianity very well at all."[16]

Our sanctification and adoption are intertwined. Sanctification means growing and learning and becoming more and more like our Father. We can pray to him at any time. We can know that he wants what is best for his children. Sometimes this growth involves suffering, and in these times we can have confidence that our Father is still there holding us up.

A. W. Tozer wrote, "He remembers our frame and knows that we are dust. He may sometimes chasten us, it is true, but even this He does with a smile, the proud, tender smile of a Father who is bursting with pleasure over an imperfect but promising son who is coming every day to look more and more like the One whose child he is."[17]

These are all biblical truths you will keep coming back to for the rest of your life. Yet we sometimes forget these foundational truths and become discouraged. This is where we must remember that once we repent and believe, we are brought into a glorious new community—the church. It is with other believers that you can be reminded of your new identity.[18]

NEW COMMUNITY

Circle back to Romans 12:1–2, from the start of this article. Notice that in this passage, Paul speaks collectively to the readers. He does not address individuals, he addresses the *community*—brothers and sisters—a family. As Paul writes, he pictures them gathered and listening to his letter together.

Here Paul is saying *I urge you* in the plural. The appropriate way to think of this plural usage is to think Southern and say *y'all*. Yes, Paul is effectively saying, "I urge y'all to present your bodies as a living sacrifice."

We call this *y'all*—this new community—by a familiar name: the church.

There are two distinct ways we become part of the church when we repent and believe the gospel and are adopted into his family. There is the *universal church* and the *local church*.

The *universal church* is the community of all true believers for all time.[19] We are not alone, but share an invisible connection with all those who confess Christ all around the world and with those believers from ages past. How awesome is that?

The *local church* is sometimes referred to as the visible church. That is because it is the gathering of Christ-followers that we can see with our mortal eyes. The book of Acts records the expansion and establishment of local churches wherever the gospel went out. Planting churches was an immediate and essential aspect of gospel proclamation.

A theology of the gospel must point us to the church. Why? All who embrace the gospel are immediately birthed into the new community of the church.

The church is our new home. Fellow believers are our new adoptive family. In the gospel, we are not just united to Christ, we are united to his church. We are called to find the believers around us and be discipled by them in order to become more like Christ.

In an age of bold individualism and autonomy, Christians in the twenty-first century need this gospel reorientation. Jesus Christ died and rose again for *us*, not simply for *me*.

"*Let us hold on to the confession of our hope* without wavering, since he who promised is faithful. *And let us watch out for one another to provoke love and good works*, not neglecting to gather together, as some are in the habit of doing, but encouraging each other, and all the more as you see the day approaching" (Hebrews 10:23–25, emphasis added).

This "confession of our hope" is the gospel. By gathering, we remember this good news together and come alongside the Holy Spirit in the sanctification process—reminding each other that God is at work as our loving Father!

APPLICATION

So far in this study, we have explored the content of the gospel message and the response to the gospel message for someone who has not yet followed Jesus. In this section, we are exploring topics that we will be living in for the rest of our lives on earth. We will always be seeking to live in accordance with our *new identity* (sanctification and adoption) and our *new community* (Christ's body, the church).

In your home, workplace, or school, how are you living in ways that do not match your new identity? What thoughts or doubts rob you of joy and distract you from remembering your privileged position as a child of God? Do you have Christian community around you to challenge and encourage you? As you seek to share the gospel with others, how will you seek to invite them into their new identity and new community?

1. How did you summarize Romans 6, 7, and 8? What were the major things you learned or noticed?

2. What is sanctification? How is sanctification a "work of God *and* man"?

3. Will we ever be completely free from the temptation to sin in this life? Why or why not?

4. How does knowing you are adopted into God's family change the way you live as a Christian today?

5. Why is it so important to be involved in a local church with other believers?

6. In your life, what are the major challenges keeping you from living out of your new identity? What keeps you from living as you should within your new community?

SURVEY

Survey three people.

ASK: What do you think of when you think of church?

Answers to this question will vary widely depending on your cultural context. Some will have personal experiences with church that have flavored their view of Christ and Christians in one way or another. Others will be leaning on the experiences of their friends or family.

Whatever the case, once again be a LISTENER. The purpose of this question is to hear where people have come from and find anchor points to connect what you have been learning to their particular situation.

RESPONSE FROM PERSON #1:

RESPONSE FROM PERSON #2:

RESPONSE FROM PERSON #3:

NOTE FOR YOURSELF: What did you learn from your survey? What connections do you see between the survey responses and the article or the Scriptures you've been studying?

SMALL GROUP MEETING

Meet with your group to share what you learned from the survey and discuss your workbook answers.

Session

8

CULMINATION

WHY THE CULMINATION MATTERS

In session 7 we studied the "already and not yet" aspect of the Christian life. We are in Christ *the moment* we repent and believe the good news. God grants us a new identity and welcomes us into a new community. But that's not the end of the story. We now journey on a new path, a new destiny, one that leads us to the gates of a kingdom God has prepared for us.

Apart from Christ, there is only hope of the world becoming marginally better. In fact, you may have friends who hold a worldview like John Lennon. In his song "Imagine," Lennon dreams of a world with no possessions, borders, religions, or heaven and hell—just a brotherhood living as one, and living for today. Somehow, if we just try hard enough to come together, there will be less injustice, less hunger, less suffering.

However, our life experience shows us that this is not what results from a bunch of people living for today. Rather, this worldview leads to blatant selfishness and greed. We saw in the garden what happens when we trust in our own human efforts to run this world!

The Christian hope is oriented in the same direction as Lennon's dream, but is much more complete. The injustice we see will be reversed by perfect justice from a loving and righteous Judge. Hunger and suffering will be no more as those who trust in Jesus all enjoy eternal life and brotherhood together with their Savior. The things Christ offers are the things your friends already hope for—but on steroids!

The world Lennon imagines is a shadow of what we are really yearning for. Our souls by nature want to get back to Shalom, life-as-it-should-be with our Creator. When we get to this new kingdom, we will say, "I have come home at last! This is my real country! I belong here. This is the land I have been looking for all my life, though I never knew it till now."[20] Catching a glimpse of our future home will have a dramatic impact on the way we live today.

***

To prepare for your small group meeting:

- Complete the reading assignment
- Read the article
- Answer the workbook questions

READING ASSIGNMENT

Read Revelation 20–22 a minimum of three times. Use a different translation each time.

- How do these final chapters of the Bible describe an epic resolution, wrapping up the story that began with Genesis? Be specific about the elements and list them below.

- Write down where you see God described as the following:
  Loving Creator

  Supreme authority

  Final Judge

When we arrive at the last scene in the book of Revelation, we discover some familiar themes from the opening pages of Genesis: an angel, a serpent, people, a restored throne, a certain tree that is no longer out of reach, and so much more. The connections to Genesis 1–3 are everywhere!

These final pages are filled with contrasts. The darkest hour in history is immediately followed by the dawn of a new day. The headlines can barely capture the force of good news contained in these pages: Enemy Is Crushed! Peace! Jesus Christ Wins! Rescue!

Two main events dominate these pages: final judgment and the re-creation of heaven and earth.

FINAL JUDGMENT

Revelation gives us a vivid picture of what the future holds when we stand before the final Judge.

> Then I saw a great white throne and one seated on it. Earth and heaven fled from his presence, and no place was found for them. I also saw the dead, the great and the small, standing before the throne, and books were opened. Another book was opened, which is the book of life, and the dead were judged according to their works by what was written in the books. Then the sea gave up the dead that were in it, and

> Death and Hades gave up the dead that were in them; each
> one was judged according to their works. Death and Hades
> were thrown into the lake of fire. This is the second death, the
> lake of fire. And anyone whose name was not found written
> in the book of life was thrown into the lake of fire. (Revela-
> tion 20:11–15)

All of history has been moving toward this day. The grand storyline of
the Bible is about to reach its climactic culmination. We've been waiting
for this day since Genesis 3!

The King sits victoriously on his throne. This is no viceroy. This is the
King of kings and Lord of lords—this is Jesus Christ. Before him stand
all who have died (that is, all people from the beginning of time). They
stand before the one who lovingly created them, holds supreme authority, and is about to execute his final judgment.

There is no deliberation. Sentencing is clear and unchallenged. How is
judgment executed? Notice the careful distinction that is made between
the books (plural) that were opened and the singular book that was
opened, identified as the Book of Life.

The stack of books contains a record of humanity's works, yours and
mine included. Everything has been recorded. *Everything.* People who
may have imagined they had escaped punishment are shocked. Rather
than getting away with it, their well-deserved punishment has been
stored up for this day (see Romans 2:5–6). Every careless word spoken
has been recorded. Everything hidden in darkness and every intention
of the heart is suddenly revealed.

These words are haunting: "Each one was judged according to their
works." The stack of books contains the complete record of every person's works, and all will stand on that day with their stunned mouths
silent, guilty as charged.

But what about this other book in Revelation 20? Look carefully. What is contained in the *Book of Life*? Is it all the good works to counterbalance all the bad works? *Nothing of the kind!* The final Judge does not bring a scale to this day. The only thing recorded in the Book of Life is a list of names.

If you are *in Christ* you don't have to fear that day. Your name is in the Book of Life! "There is now no condemnation for those in Christ Jesus" (Romans 8:1). As far as the east is from the west, God has removed our condemnation from us. Instead of condemnation on that day, those whose names are recorded in the Book of Life are welcomed into "a new heaven and a new earth" (Revelation 21:1). God brings his children home. No more death. No more sin. No more crying or pain. All that is gone. Forever.

We need to let those words sink deep into our souls. We have never lived in a world with no more death. What will it be like to never fear death? Reminders of death are everywhere—both the sudden, shocking kinds of death as well as the slow, agonizing kinds of death. Oh, to live in that place where death is *absent*!

Wait—no more *sin* either? It is gone from my life, gone from my desires, gone from everyone else in the entire world. Astounding! Glorious! Whatever crying or pain came as a result of death and sin—gone. Forever gone. We are in a whole new world.

And here is the most unimaginable part: Have you ever thought, *Man, I wonder what it would have been like to walk and talk with Jesus when he was here*? Well, you'll get that chance! And he is in no hurry. Jesus will be the first one to welcome you into this incredible new home. HOME! And the best part of going home is always the family we get to share it with. That will especially be true of this homecoming—especially seeing the one who gave his life to get us there.

I can't wait.

The message of the gospel must go out to all. It is an appeal to people to prepare for their day in court. Are you prepared to stand before the final Judge? Your name is either in the book or it is not. You are either "in Christ" or you are not. You are either guilty in your sin or you are forgiven and free. "Look, I am coming soon," Jesus tells us (see 2 Corinthians 5:17; Romans 6:6–11; John 5:24; Colossians 1:13–14).

NEW HEAVEN AND NEW EARTH

Then Jesus looks over all of his redeemed people and with unrestrained joy cries, "Look, I am making everything new" (Revelation 21:5). Oh, and remember that tree Adam and Eve were guarded from after they sinned? What was the name of the tree? Look at Revelation 22:1–2. "Then he showed me the river of the water of life, clear as crystal, flowing from the throne of God and of the Lamb down the middle of the city's main street. The tree of life was on each side of the river, bearing twelve kinds of fruit, producing its fruit every month."

The tree of life is alive, breathtaking, and of colossal proportions! It spans a whole river and produces more and more incredible fruit every month to keep us coming back!

What will we do in this new heaven and new earth? Do you recall what God wanted from the beginning? Adam was to rule and reign over a perfect garden as God's viceroy. Check out Revelation 22:5. "And they will reign forever and ever." All is as it should be. Eden is restored. And we get to be there.

I hope the culmination of the eternal gospel fills you with awe, worship, and deep gratitude. I also hope it fills you with an incredible desire to tell others what you have found.

APPLICATION

I'll never forget reading the story of young Jim Elliot when I was a new believer. Elliot was so compelled by the gospel that he was willing to risk everything in order to get the good news out to all people. In fact, he paid the ultimate price to do just that. This quote from his journal says it all: "Father, make of me a crisis man. Bring those I contact to decision. Let me not be a milepost on a single road; make me a fork, that men must turn one way or another on facing Christ in me."[21]

Once you encounter the eternal gospel, you must tell others. And when you do so, invite the hearer toward a course of action. The gospel provokes a decision.

May the eternal gospel captivate your soul and ignite a passion in you to proclaim it to the ends of the earth.

Amen.

Session

WORKBOOK

1. How do the final chapters of the Bible describe an epic resolution to the story of the Bible?

2. Often great stories will tie together themes and ideas brought up in the beginning at the end. What do you see in this passage that reminds you of the beginning pages of Genesis?

3. What strikes you about the judgment scene? Why is it so important to understand the difference between the books and the Book of Life?

4. Look in Revelation again to see the words used to describe heaven. This seems to be a very real and tangible place! How does the biblical picture of heaven clash with the popular view of heaven?

5. This is a beautiful picture of the new kingdom that we will experience as followers of Christ. How can we contribute to God's kingdom while we wait for this ultimate ending?

SMALL GROUP MEETING

Meet with your group to discuss your workbook answers and what you have learned from this course.

ENDNOTES

1. Randy Raysbrook, "One-Verse Evangelism," *Discipleship Journal* 34 (1986): 28.

2. D. A. Carson, "The Biblical Gospel," in *For Such a Time as This: Perspectives on Evangelicalism, Past, Present and Future,* ed. Steve Brady and Harold Rowdon (London: Scripture Union/Evangelical Alliance, 1996), 75–85.

3. John Calvin, *Institutes of the Christian Religion*, trans. Floyd Lewis Battles (Philadelphia: Westminster, 1960), 1:108.

4. Timothy Keller, *The Prodigal God* (New York: Dutton, 2008), 43.

5. For a great summary of the eternal gospel in the form of a children's book, check out *The Biggest Story: How the Snake Crusher Brings Us Back to the Garden* (Wheaton, IL: Crossway, 2015) by Kevin DeYoung.

6. Wayne Grudem, *Systematic Theology: An Introduction to Biblical Doctrine* (Grand Rapids, MI: Zondervan, 1994), 723.

7. R. C. Sproul's use of the three circles can be found, for example, in *The Truth of the Cross* (Lake Mary, FL: Reformation Trust, 2007), 85–95.

8. For an amazing lecture on this topic, please consider watching R. C. Sproul, "The Center of Christian Preaching: Justification by Faith" (presented at Together for the Gospel, Louisville, KY, 2006), https://vimeo.com/103906718.

9. C. J. Mahaney, *The Cross-Centered Life: Keeping the Gospel the Main Thing* (Colorado Springs: Multnomah, 2002), 25.

10. This is an adaptation of a story once told by Fred Barshaw, an elder at Grace Community Church in Sun Valley, CA. He had a gift for creating incredible parables, allegorical stories with deep biblical themes running through them.

11. David Platt uses this illustration in *Radical: Taking Back Your Faith from the American Dream* (Colorado Springs: Multnomah, 2010).

12. John Stott, *Basic Christianity* (Downers Grove, IL: InterVarsity, 1971), 110.

13. Grudem, *Systematic Theology*, 746.

14. See, for example, "Free in Christ Jesus: A Sermon on Romans 6:11," Martyn Lloyd-Jones Trust, https://www.mljtrust.org/sermons-online/romans-6-11/free-in-christ-jesus/.

15. Grudem, *Systematic Theology*, 736.

16. J. I. Packer, *Knowing God* (Downers Grove, IL: InterVarsity, 1973), 182.

17. A. W. Tozer, *The Root of the Righteous* (Chicago: Moody, reprinted 2015), 20.

18. I could write a whole book on the importance of the gospel to our identity and in our community. Instead, I will introduce you to these concepts and refer you to Robert H. Thune and Will Walker's resources, *The Gospel-Centered Life* (Greensboro, NC: New Growth, 2011) and *The Gospel-Centered Community* (2013). These companion resources have been so helpful both personally and in the context of leading within a local church.

19. Grudem, *Systematic Theology*, 853.

20. This is one of my favorite lines from C. S. Lewis's series of books, *The Chronicles of Narnia*. It comes from the final pages of the epic concluding book in the set, *The Last Battle* (New York: HarperTrophy, 2002), 213.

21. Jim Elliot journal entry quoted by Elisabeth Elliot, *Shadow of the Almighty: The Life and Testament of Jim Elliot* (Grand Rapids, MI: Zondervan, 1989), 59.